WANDERSTATE

WELCOME TO
ARIZONA

ADVENTURE GUIDE & JOURNAL

ARIZONA BUCKET LIST

by: WANDERSTATE

Original title: Arizona Bucket List Adventure Guide & Journal

Written by: Wanderstate

Typesetting and text makeup by: Wanderstate

Paperback ISBN: 979-8446908127

Printed in the United States of America

First Edition

YOUR FREE GIFT

As a way of saying thanks for your purchase, we offer you another book (just as valuable as this book), "100 Campsites of a Lifetime America's Best Camping Adventures" completely free.

SCAN THE QR-CODE BELOW TO RECEIVE IT:

In "100 Campsites of a Lifetime", you'll have the ultimate U.S. Camping Bucket List Book that helps you plan your adventures & document the memories of a lifetime for a lifetime!

In addition to getting "100 Campsites of a Lifetime", you'll also have an opportunity to get our new books for free, enter giveaways, and receive other valuable emails from us.

AGAIN, YOU CAN SCAN THE QR-CODE ABOVE OR GO TO:

wanderstatepublishing.com

If you have any questions, suggestions for us or want to work with us, shoot us an email at:

support@wanderstatepublishing.com

INTRODUCTION

Welcome to your very own adventure guide to exploring the best destinations in Arizona. Imagine you discover, learn and save the memories of your adventures in Arizona with one book! Whether you've been to Arizona a thousand times or you're headed there for the first time, there are destinations that simply shouldn't be missed, and this what makes Arizona an adventurer's dreamland. From the North Country's pine-forested rim that drops into the depths of the Grand Canyon to the picturesque Sonoran Desert landscape of central and southern Arizona, all the ingredients for the quintessential American adventure recipe are at your fingertips.

But with so many diverse destinations in Arizona, it can be hard to pick which place is right for your next outdoor adventure.

That's why the Wanderstate team before producing Arizona Bucket List Adventure Guide & Journal, took into account several factors, including the variety of attractions, as well as the opinions of experts and travelers, to determine the best places to visit in Arizona. And testing with different readers the best format of the journal pages possible that can cover all your memories.

ADVENTURE GUIDE:
The travel guide contains the most important and popular attractions for each destination - with all the information you must know about it. We avoided putting the Fees or any other expenses. Why? Because nowadays we are in a fast-changing world, we can't tell you how much the fees are gonna be in each place, because it is an ever-changing factor. To ensure our customers have a great experience with the book we avoided putting it within this book.

DOCUMENT YOUR EXPERIENCES:
Next to every destination will be a blank page to let you document and rate your experience with information such as how was the weather when you visited the place and in what season, the trip companions, special memories, the best sights, and additional space when you can write your thoughts and notes. A place to attach more photos, stamps, tickets, emblems, and passports in case of National Parks. And of course, a space where you can rate the overall experience.

GPS COORDINATES:
Each destination contains specific GPS coordinates, For those that are not associated with the specific location, it is easiest to map it using GPS coordinates. Luckily, Google has a system of codes that converts the coordinates into pindrop locations that Google Maps is able to interpret and navigate.

THE STATE OF ARIZONA

Arizona, the Grand Canyon state, achieved statehood on February 14, 1912, the last of the 48 coterminous United States to be admitted to the union. Originally part of Spanish and Mexican territories, the land was ceded to the United States in 1848 and became a separate territory in 1863. Copper was discovered in 1854, and copper mining was Arizona's premier industry until the 1950s. After World War II, the widespread availability of refrigeration and air conditioning caused Arizona's population to boom and Phoenix to become one of the fastest-growing cities in America. Arizona is the sixth largest state in the country in terms of area. Its population has always been predominantly urban, particularly since the mid-20th century, when urban and suburban areas began growing rapidly at the expense of the countryside. Some scholars believe that the state's name comes from a Basque phrase meaning "place of oaks" while others attribute it to a Tohono O'odham (Papago) Indian phrase meaning "place of the young (or little) spring."

**Date of Statehood:** February 14, 1912
**Did you know?** Arizona has the greatest percentage of its acreage designated as Indian tribal land in the United States.
**Capital:** Phoenix
**Population:** 7,200,017 (2021)
**Size:** 113,990 square miles
**Nickname(s):** Grand Canyon State
**Motto:** Ditat Deus ("God enriches")

CONTENTS

NATIONAL PARKS / NATIONAL MONUMENTS
STATE PARKS   11

WELCOME

Arizona

LAKES / WATERFALLS / HIKES 81

OTHER POINTS OF INTEREST 123

NATIONAL PARKS
NATIONAL MONUMENTS
STATE PARKS

Arizona is home to some of the world's most breathtaking scenery, and it also boasts some impressive ruins and ancient fossils. Much of it is protected within the state's national parks, monuments, and a lot of state parks, including these seventeen fabulous places. So be sure to put at least some of these on your must-experience list.

PLAN IT | DO IT | JOURNAL IT

GRAND CANYON
36.1069° N, 112.1129° W

Established on February 26, 1919. Grand Canyon National Park, located in northwestern Arizona, is the 15th site in the United States to have been named as a national park. The park's central feature is the Grand Canyon, a gorge of the Colorado River, which is often considered one of the Wonders of the World. The park covers 1,217,262 acres (1,901.972 sq mi; 4,926.08 km2) of unincorporated areas in Coconino and Mohave counties.

BEST TIMES TO VISIT:

The best times to visit the Grand Canyon are March through May and September through November, when daytime temperatures are cool and crowds are thin. If you decide to visit during the summer (the park's peak season), be prepared for hordes of tourists and very limited lodging availability.

BEST THINGS TO DO IN GRAND CANYON NATIONAL PARK:

1. Visitor Center & Mather Point Overlook: If you are entering the park at the South Entrance, from the direction of Williams, the best thing to do is head directly to the visitor center. A few displays show a brief overview of the park and a little about the history. From the visitor center, a short path leads to Mather Point Overlook, where there are a couple of large viewing areas on a peninsula jutting out into the canyon, with great vistas over the canyon.

2. Rim Trail: This nearly level path, with a mix of sun and shade from scattered trees, is one of the most scenic walks in North America. The Rim Trail is a mostly paved walking path that follows the rim of the Grand Canyon for 13 miles. It runs from South Kaibab Trailhead, east of the Visitor Center, to Hermit's Rest, at the far west end of Hermit Road. You can access it in front of the visitor center at Mather Point, in the

Village, or from any of the scenic stops along Hermit Road.

3. **Geological Museum:** One of the most interesting and informative exhibits in Grand Canyon is the Geological Museum.

4. **Hermit Road Drive:** Hermit Road is a seven-mile scenic drive along the canyon rim, with numerous viewpoints. This is the most popular route in the park.

5. **Bright Angel Hiking Trail:** The most popular hike in the park is the Bright Angel Hike, which departs from the Village, where the shuttle bus to Hermit's Rest begins its route. This is a long hike, but many people choose to walk down the trail only a short distance to get a feel for the hike. The complete route, round-trip to Bright Angel Campground, is 19 miles and takes two days.

6. **Desert View Drive:** While most people tend to gravitate towards Hermit Road, the 22-mile Desert View Drive is equally, if not more stunning.

7. **Skywalk & Eagle Point:** You can reach it in about a four-hour drive from the South Rim. This horseshoe-shaped glass walkway extends out 70 feet over the canyon, allowing you to peer straight down. You can also dine at the Sky View restaurant and look out over the Skywalk. and visiting the Native American Village.

There are many other attractions such as Desert View Watchtower, Lookout Studio and the Kolb Gallery, Wildlife Viewing, IMAX Movie at the National Geographic Visitor Center, Nearby - Little Colorado River Overlook.

GRAND CANYON TOURS:

1. **Helicopter Flight over the Grand Canyon:** If you want to fully appreciate the grandeur of the Grand Canyon, take a 25-minute Grand Canyon Helicopter Tour and soar out over the abyss to get a bird's-eye view.

2. **Grand Canyon White Water Rafting Trip from Las Vegas:** Raft 40 miles of the Colorado River on a one-day Grand Canyon White Water Rafting Trip leaving from Las Vegas.

3. **South Rim Mule Rides:** Mule rides are offered year-round from the South Rim. The mules carry guests down the Bright Angel Trail on a 5.5-hour trip for an overnight stay at Phantom Ranch and then return the next day.

« Travel makes one modest. You see what a tiny place you occupy in the world. »
- Gustave Flaubert

DATE(S) VISITED:

WEATHER:

☐ ☐ ☐ ☐ ☐

SEASON:

☐ ☐ ☐ ☐

COMPANIONS:

_____
_____
_____

SPECIAL MEMORIES:

_____
_____
_____
_____
_____
_____
_____
_____
_____

SIGHTS:

_____
_____
_____
_____
_____
_____
_____
_____

NOTES:

_____
_____
_____
_____
_____
_____
_____
_____
_____
_____
_____

PHOTOS, STAMPS:

RATING: / 10   **WILL RETURN?** YES / NO

PETRIFIED FOREST
35.0037° N, 109.7889° W

Established on December 9, 1962. Petrified Forest National Park, named for its high concentration of rainbow-colored petrified wood, is located in Apache County and Navajo County in northeastern Arizona. The fee area of the park covers approximately 230 square miles and it is almost 30 miles long from north to south. The park receives around 650,000 recreational visitors each year for sightseeing, photography, hiking, and backpacking. Petrified Forest is also a popular stop along with road trips- it's located along the iconic Route 66 (so it's literally on the way from Flagstaff to Albuquerque or vice versa) and close to popular attractions in Arizona, like Sedona and the Grand Canyon. The Southwestern United States is the perfect place to go on an epic road trip- and Petrified Forest is a totally not-to-be-missed spot. You will need a car to explore Petrified Forest National Park since there is no public transportation to the park or shuttle service through it.

BEST TIMES TO VISIT:
The fall is a lovely time to visit the park with less visitation, milder temperatures, and normally less precipitation.

A QUICK GUIDE TO VISITING PETRIFIED FOREST NATIONAL PARK:
The park has one main artery. If you enter from I-40 and drive the entire 28 miles, you will end up at the Rainbow Forest Museum, just off Highway 180. If you enter from Highway 180, you will end near I-40. From the Rainbow Forest Museum, it is approximately a 25-minute drive to return to Heber and I-40. From Phoenix, head north on I-17 to Flagstaff, and go east on I-40. Watch for exit 311. If you are starting from the East Valley in the Greater Phoenix metropolitan area, you can take Highway 87 north to Payson. Turn right on Highway 260 to Heber, and then take 377 towards Holbrook.

ust before entering Holbrook, turn right on Highway 180. From Albuquerque, take
-40 west to exit 311.

'etrified Forest National Park has two visitor centers on either end of the 28-mile
nain park road. Since Painted Desert Visitor Center is just off I-40 at exit 311, most
'isitors begin their trip with the 18-minute orientation film there. The Rainbow
'orest Museum, which serves as the southern entrance's visitor center, contains
)aleontological exhibits, including prehistoric animal skeletons. Most visitors choose
o explore the park by car, but you can also cycle along the park's 28 paved miles, or
explore the backcountry on horseback.

3est Hikes & Trails: Several trails start at the Rainbow Forest Museum parking lot,
nost of which are under 2 miles. There is a shelter at the intersection of this trail and
he Long Logs trail if you need to sit in the shade and both trails can be combined for
i 2.6-mile hike.

.. Giant Logs Loop: This .4-mile loop features Old Faithful—a 10-foot-wide petrified
og, as well as other large, tree-shaped blocks of quartz.

2. Long Logs: You can take this a 1.6-mile loop through one of the park's highest
concentrations of fossilized logs.

3. Agate House Trail: This two-mile trail leads to an eight-room pueblo constructed
of petrified wood, which stands on top of a small hill.
4. Blue Mesa Trail: One of the most scenic spots in the park—tinged blue, purple,
and gray by bentonite clay—this mile-long loop takes you through the badlands on a
paved and gravel trail.
5. Puerco Pueblo: Stretch your legs by walking the 0.3-mile, paved trail to see the
knee-high remains of the pueblo's 100-plus rooms
See Native American Petroglyphs: This brings us seamlessly to the next of these
things to do in Petrified Forest National Park. Near Puerco Pueblo, a 0.3-mile
(500-meter) hiking trail leads to a couple of overlooks where you can see petroglyphs.
See the Old Studebaker on Old Route 66: When driving the park's main road
southward, you'll intersect Old Route 66 shortly after leaving the Painted Desert rim.

« Fear is only temporary. Regrets last forever. »
- Unknown

DATE(S) VISITED:

WEATHER:

☐ ☐ ☐ ☐ ☐

SEASON:

☐ ☐ ☐ ☐

COMPANIONS: _____

_____

_____

_____

SPECIAL MEMORIES: _____

_____

_____

_____

_____

_____

_____

_____

_____

SIGHTS: _____

_____

_____

_____

_____

_____

_____

_____

_____

NOTES: _____

_____

_____

_____

_____

_____

_____

_____

_____

_____

_____

PHOTOS, STAMPS:

RATING: / 10	WILL RETURN? YES / NO

SAGUARO
32.2967° N, 111.1666° W

Established on October 14, 1994. Saguaro National Park is one of America's few national parks dedicated to protecting one plant. Saguaros are plants with personalities. They often look human, standing tall and proud, their arms reaching toward the sky or pointing the way. Though some achieve heights of 50 feet and weigh up to 8 tons, saguaros grow slowly. It usually takes 15 years for them to reach 1 foot in height, and they don't flower or produce fruit until they're about 30. They take about 100 years to reach a height of 25 feet. Their maximum life span is about 200 years. The park consists of two separate sections. The Tucson Mountain District, also called Saguaro West, covers 32 square miles of Sonoran Desert west of Tucson; the Rincon Mountain District, also called Saguaro East, covers 104 square miles of saguaro forest, desert, foothills, and mountain terrain on the east side of Tucson. The two sections are about 30 miles apart.

Tips: A visit to Saguaro National Park West may be combined with visits to the Arizona-Sonora Desert Museum (2.6 miles from the Red Hills Visitor Center) and Old Tucson (5.6 miles from the Red Hills Visitor Center). Saguaro West (Tucson Mountain District) – More dense cacti with one of the best overlooks but is also more crowded with people.
Saguaro East (Rincon Mountain District) – Closer to the mountains, so you will get pretty saguaro silhouettes against a purple mountain backdrop.

BEST TIMES TO VISIT:
Summers are hot and winters comfortable, so the best time to visit, especially for hikers, is between October and April.

A QUICK GUIDE TO VISITING SAGUARO NATIONAL PARK:

You can explore Saguaro in so many ways from scenic drives to hiking, and watching the sunset. Please note that Saguaro National Park West/Tucson Mountain District is in the Tucson Mountain Range and borders Marana. Saguaro West is where the architecturally stunning Red Hills Visitor Center is located (at 2700 N Kinney Rd., Tucson). During regular operations, the Red Hills Visitor Center offers guided tours, indoor exhibits, gift shops, restrooms, vending machines, and drinking fountains.

1. Scenic Drives: Tour the Bajada Loop Drive in Saguaro National Park West for a great overview of the park and sweeping mountain, and valley views. Everywhere you look, you'll see hillsides studded with majestic saguaro cacti. Stop at a picnic area or trailhead to get out and explore on foot.

2. Go Hiking & Have a Picnic: The park offers more than 165 miles of trails. On the western side of the park, the Valley View Overlook Trail is a popular choice offering a short hike with a stunning scenic view. In Saguaro National West, Signal Hill Picnic Area is a one-of-a-kind place to picnic. There are a number of covered picnic tables to choose from, each having a spectacular view of near and far rocks, mountains, and vistas. It's an easy half-mile hike up a gentle hill and this trail rewards hikers with dozens of ancient petroglyphs. Another popular choice is the Valley View Trail, which

offers gorgeous views of Avra Valley and Picacho Peak to the north. There are picnic areas along Golden Gate Road, all nestled into the Saguaro Cactus landscape that is famous worldwide.

3. View Ancient Petroglyphs: You can view a solar spiral petroglyph, and many others in Saguaro National Park West by following the Signal Hill Trail.

4. Mountain Biking: The Bajada Loop Drive on the West side of the park is a six-mile gravel path, perfect for mountain bikes.

5. Camping Trip: Backcountry camping is available to backpackers only (no vehicles or RV camping is permitted). There is a Pima county-maintained park in Tucson Mountain Park, a couple of B&Bs, and private campsites in the vicinity of Saguaro National Park West. There are six campgrounds throughout Saguaro National Park East/Rincon Mountains, and a permit is required for all camping stays.

« Stop being afraid of what could go wrong,
and start being excited of what could go right. »
- Tony Robbins

DATE(S) VISITED:

WEATHER:

☐ ☐ ☐ ☐ ☐

SEASON:

☐ ☐ ☐ ☐

COMPANIONS: _____

_____

_____

_____

SPECIAL MEMORIES: _____

_____

_____

_____

_____

_____

_____

_____

_____

SIGHTS: _____

_____

_____

_____

_____

_____

_____

_____

NOTES: _____

_____

_____

_____

_____

_____

_____

_____

_____

_____

PHOTOS, STAMPS:

RATING: / 10	WILL RETURN? YES / NO

CANYON DE CHELLY
36.1336° N, 109.4694° W

In the state of Arizona, near its eastern edge, Canyon de Chelly (pronounced "de-SHAY") National Monument rewards intrepid travelers with spectacular views and glimpses into traditional Native American life. Chinle, AZ is best known as the gateway to Canyon de Chelly National Monument, an 84,000-acre site that preserves large collections of significant Ancestral Pueblo, Hopi, and Navajo ruins. You can view Ancestral Puebloan pit houses dating back nearly 5,000 years, cliff dwellings built into the canyon walls, and Hogans lived in by Navajo from overlooks on the rim. However, to explore the canyons' interior, you'll need to hire a Navajo guide. Navajo Nation tour guides offer a variety of guided tours of the area's natural and historical attractions, including the ruins of the area's canyons, the Navajo National Zoological and Botanical Park, and the Window Rock Monument. Certain attractions may be temporarily closed or require advance reservations.

BEST TIMES TO VISIT:
The best time to visit the Canyon de Chelly area, are the spring months of April and May, the summer months (June, July, and August), and the autumn months of September and October.

A QUICK GUIDE TO VISITING CANYON DE CHELLY N. MONUMENT:
The visitor center and several overlooks—Massacre Cave Overlook on North Rim Drive, Tsegi, Junction, White House, and Spider Rock overlooks on South Rim Drive—are accessible. Backcountry trails and areas are not.

Most people experience the park by driving its two scenic drives, one with views of Canyon de Chelly and the other with views of Canyon del Muerto. Stop by the visitor enter to pick up a map, watch the 23-minute introductory video, and learn about ranger-led programs before hitting the road. You can also hire a Navajo guide at the visitor center to take you into the canyon on a 4x4, horseback, or hiking tour.

Scenic Drives: Of the park's two scenic drives, the South Rim Drive is the most popular. Following the edge of Canyon de Chelly, it boasts one of the park's most notable formations, Spider Rock, an 800-foot sandstone monolith said to be the home of Spider-Woman. But the North Rim Drive is equally impressive with views of Canyon del Muerto.

Canyon Tours: Except for the White House Trail, you can only access the canyon with a ranger or a Navajo guide. Most tour companies offer 4x4 tours, guided hikes, and overnight camping.

4x4 tours: Usually conducted in Jeeps, these tours range from three to eight hours.

Horseback riding: Justin's Horse Rental takes visitors on guided horseback rides into the canyons.

Best Hikes & Trails: There is only one trail in Canyon de Chelly National Monument that you can hike without a guide, the White House Trail. If you want to explore any further, you'll either need to take a ranger-led hike or hire a Navajo guide. Trails you can hike with a guide include Beehive, Bat, Tunnel, Bear, Baby, Crow, and White

Sands. **White House Trail:** This 2.5-mile, out-and-back trail starts at the White House Overlook on South Rim Drive and switchbacks 600 feet down to the canyon floor, ending at the White House Ruin.

Where to Camp: There are two campgrounds in the area. The first is located near the visitor center and managed by Navajo Nation Parks and Recreation while the other is privately operated by a Navajo guide on his property near the Spider Rock Overlook.

* Note: Pets are not permitted in the visitor center, on the White House Trail, or canyon tours. However, your leashed pet can accompany you at the overlooks and in the campground.

« *The real voyage of discovery consists not in seeking new landscapes, but in having new eyes.* »
- Marcel Proust

DATE(S) VISITED:

WEATHER:

☐ ☐ ☐ ☐ ☐

SEASON:

☐ ☐ ☐ ☐

COMPANIONS: _____

_____

_____

_____

SPECIAL MEMORIES: _____

_____

_____

_____

_____

_____

_____

_____

SIGHTS: _____

_____

_____

_____

_____

_____

_____

_____

_____

NOTES:

_____
_____
_____
_____
_____
_____
_____
_____
_____
_____

PHOTOS, STAMPS:

RATING: / 10   WILL RETURN?   YES / NO

MONUMENT VALLEY
36.9969° N, 110.0986° W

Straddling the Arizona/Utah border, Monument Valley is one of the nation's most recognizable landscapes, The three red sandstone buttes that mark the horizon of Monument Valley have now become a symbol of the ideal of the American Far West (great Hollywood westerns were shot there), movies like "Forrest Gump," access is restricted within the park. While you can drive a 17-mile section through the park on your own, you'll need a Navajo guide to do anything more than that. However, that's part of what makes Monument Valley so unique—you learn about Navajo history, culture, and traditions from the tribal member welcoming you into their lands.

BEST TIMES TO VISIT:
Monument Valley is open and can be visited year-round and each season can obviously present, as expected, both pros and cons, but nothing that would prevent you from enjoying the beauty of the site. The best seasons are spring and fall, when, thanks to favorable temperatures, your visit will be more enjoyable.

A QUICK GUIDE TO VISITING MONUMENT VALLEY NAVAJO TRIBAL PARK:
Monument Valley is quite remote, the nearest major cities of Phoenix and Albuquerque are both roughly 320 miles away. From Phoenix, take I-17 north to I-40. Head east to the edge of Flagstaff, and follow signs to pick up US-89 north. Drive approximately 70 miles and turn at US-160, heading east towards Tuba City. Follow this to Kayenta. Turn north on US-163 and continue 25 miles to the park's entrance. From Albuquerque, take 1-40 west to Gallup. At Gallup, head north on US-491. Before leaving Gallup, turn left onto SR 264 and head west to Burnside. There, take US 191 north and drive 40 miles north to Indian Route 59. Where IR-59 intersects US-160, turn left. Go 8 miles,

nd turn right at US-163. Head north 25 miles to the park's entrance. If you're short
n time, drive the 17-mile, extremely rough dirt road past the Mittens and Totem Pole
ormations on a self-guided tour. If you have more time, book a tour with a Navajo
uide online or at the park's visitor center. Tours range from 90 minutes to full-day
dventures. Some guides even offer traditional meals, entertainment, and overnight
tays in a Hogan. Beyond that, activities are limited in the park. There are no ranger-
ed programs, helicopter rides, or hot air balloon rides there. You can't mountain bike,
ff-road, or ride your own horse through the park either.

* Note: Drones, weapons, and alcohol are prohibited on Navajo land. Because
the monuments are considered sacred, you are not allowed to climb them.

Hiking in Monument Valley: The Wildcat Trail is the only one you can hike
nescorted in Monument Valley. If you want to do anything more, you'll have to hire
. Navajo guide. Book a hiking tour before you go. Otherwise, there's no guarantee a
uide at the visitor center will be available—or prepared—to take you on a hike when
ou arrive. This 3.2-mile trail begins at the campground next to The View Hotel and
oops around the Left Mitten before returning. Go at sunrise. Not only is it cooler, but
he soft light washes the valley in ever-changing color.

Types of Tours: Most people experience Monument Valley on a 4x4 tour, but there
are other options, including horseback rides and photography tours, Overnight
Tours, Cultural Tours, and Basic Scenic tours. Each Navajo guide or company offers
slightly different tours.

Where to Camp: You can camp inside the park at The View Campground. Nearby,
camping is also available at Goulding's RV & Campgrounds and Monument Valley
KOA.

« Traveling allows you to become so many different versions of yourself. »
- Unknown

DATE(S) VISITED:

WEATHER:

☐ ☐ ☐ ☐ ☐

SEASON:

☐ ☐ ☐ ☐

COMPANIONS:

_____

_____

_____

SPECIAL MEMORIES:

_____

_____

_____

_____

_____

_____

_____

_____

SIGHTS:

_____

_____

_____

_____

_____

_____

_____

_____

NOTES: _____

_____

_____

_____

_____

_____

_____

_____

_____

_____

PHOTOS, STAMPS:

RATING: / 10   **WILL RETURN?**   YES / NO

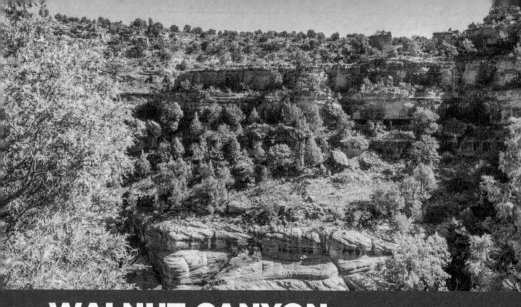

WALNUT CANYON
35.1690° N, 111.5043° W

Walnut Canyon National Monument is one of the area's most impressive attractions, both for culture and scenery. Located just outside of Flagstaff, Arizona, Walnut Canyon National Monument contains 232 prehistoric sites dating back to the 1100s. The area was once home to the Sinagua people, who built more than 80 cliff dwellings in the span of hundreds of years. After pot-hunters dynamited many of these dwellings in search of artifacts in the 1800s, President Woodrow Wilson established the national monument in 1915 to preserve what was left.1 Today, only 25 cliff dwellings line the monument's trails, but they provide a glimpse into ancient canyon life. Ancient Sinagua cliff dwellings line the steep canyon walls, which descend to the narrow and dry Walnut Creek at the bottom.

BEST TIMES TO VISIT:

The best time to visit Walnut Canyon National Monument is between September and November when the trees are alight with color and the weather is crisp and clear.

A QUICK GUIDE TO VISITING WALNUT CANYON N. MONUMENT:

At the visitor center, two accessible lifts provide entry to the park's museum, gift shop, and indoor and outdoor observation areas. The restrooms are also accessible. On the trails, options are limited. The Rim Trail is wheelchair-accessible up to the first overlook, approximately 150 feet. Beyond that point, it does not fully meet ADA accessibility standards. However, because the trail is relatively flat, some may be able to manage it with assistance. Ask at the visitor center about the possibility of continuing before setting out on the trail. The Island Trail is not accessible due to its steepness and 736 stairs.

Walnut Canyon National Monument is just 7.5 miles east of downtown Flagstaff. To get there from I-40, take Exit 204 and drive 3 miles south to the visitor center.

Activities at Walnut Canyon National Monument focus on the cliff dwellings. The visitor center museum features several exhibits on the Sinagua people and displays the artifacts they left behind. You can also watch a 20-minute introductory film on Walnut Canyon's history, while kids can pick up a Junior Ranger booklet and complete the activities. Ruins can be seen at a distance from the visitor center, but to get the best views, take a self-guided hike along the rim or into the canyon. The park also offers ranger-led discovery hikes, which require advance reservations, and daily ranger talks. Additionally, every March, local archaeologists celebrate Arizona Archaeology and Heritage Awareness month with events, lectures, walks, and activities for kids. While you're on a hike on one of the well-carved trails, you'll find photography opportunities at every bend. Either through your photo lens or your binoculars, expect wildlife. Since there's minimal human development and a source of water, animals have created an ecosystem there. You might spot coyotes, mule deer, rabbits, squirrels, and more. There's also an abundance of birds at least 121 species.

Best Hikes & Trails: The park has two self-guided trails: the Rim Trail and the Island

Trail. As its name suggests, the Rim Trail hugs the rim of the canyon, while the Island Trail descends into the canyon and takes you past cliff dwellings.

Where to Camp: There is no camping at Walnut Canyon National Monument, but you'll find several public campgrounds in Coconino National Forest. Most of the forest service campgrounds are seasonal, so check before you go if you plan to visit during the winter.

* Note: Do not touch, climb, or lean on the cliff dwellings. Leave rocks, plants, and anything else you find as they are. Don't feed any animals you encounter.

« We travel, initially, to lose ourselves; and we travel, next to find ourselves. »
- Pico Iyer

DATE(S) VISITED:

WEATHER:

☐ ☐ ☐ ☐ ☐

SEASON:

☐ ☐ ☐ ☐

COMPANIONS:

SPECIAL MEMORIES:

SIGHTS:

NOTES:

PHOTOS, STAMPS:

RATING: / 10   WILL RETURN?   YES / NO

CHIRICAHUA
32.0136° N, 109.3423° W

Known as the "Wonderland of Rocks", Chiricahua National Monument is a geologic marvel located in a remote region of Southern Arizona. It is home to an unusual collection of balanced rocks, columns, and pinnacles (or "standing-up rocks" as they were known to the native Chiricahua Apache). The otherworldly display you'll discover in Chiricahua NM was formed by the eruption of the Turkey Creek Volcano which sprayed ash over 1200 square miles. As the super-heated ash melted together, they formed rock layers known as rhyolite which then cooled and cracked. Millions of years of ice, water, wind, and erosion enlarged the cracks, forming the beautiful landscape you see today. It is also worth noting that the monument was designated as an International Dark Sky Park in April 2021, which means it is a fantastic place for stargazers and astrophotographers to photograph the milky way and star-filled skies.

BEST TIMES TO VISIT:

Chiricahua National Monument enjoys fairly mild weather year-round. Spring is the optimal time to visit, with high temperatures ranging from the mid-60s in March to the low-80s in May. Autumn is also mild, with highs reaching the mid-80s in September and the mid-70s in October.

BEST THINGS TO DO IN CHIRICAHUA NATIONAL MONUMENT:

1. Heart of Rocks: If you're an average traveler who would like to get the most bang for their buck, be sure to check out the Heart of Rocks Loop. Stemming off from the Lower Rhyolite Canyon and Sarah Deming trails, the Heart of Rocks Loop is an easy walk that shows off many of the most unusual rock formations in the monument. This trail will take you up close to see a wide array of the famous rock formations Chiricahua is known for, including several examples of the mind-bending balanced

ocks.

Massai Point: Massai Point is your must-hit destination. This vista point allows visitors a 360-degree panoramic view to gaze deep into the canyons and out into the distance. Not only is this high plateau accessible by roads and trails, but Chiricahua National Monument also offers a free shuttle that will drop you steps away. If you'd like to drive yourself to Massai Point, we can't recommend the Bonita Canyon Scenic Route enough. This eight-mile paved road will take you right to Massai Point. However, the journey is just as enjoyable as the destination! You will come across multiple pullouts to enjoy the scenery as you drive.

Faraway Ranch Historic District: You've got to visit Faraway Ranch Historic District to get the full picture of what life was like for the settlers who lived their lives in Chiricahua National Monument almost two centuries ago. there, you will get the opportunity to step inside the historic Faraway House, which was the home of the Erickson family. This Swedish immigrant family created an entire ranch to host and entertain guests. Many of these structures, as well as a historic cemetery, the Stafford family cabin, work barns, and a horse corral, are still standing today for visitors to admire while they ponder the lives of these people that lived there long ago. For those who really want to dig deep into the history, we recommend taking a guided tour of the Faraway Ranch Historic District with a park ranger.

Picnicking: The Bonita Creek and Faraway picnic areas have tables, grills, trashcans, and restrooms. Massai Point, Echo Canyon, and Sugarloaf areas have tables and restrooms. Water is available at Faraway Ranch and the visitor center. Picnicking in Bonita Canyon campground is prohibited.

A visit to Chiricahua National Monument offers a range of activities and attractions. There is something for everyone. The park's mild climate is suitable for a wide variety of outdoor activities throughout most of the year: day hiking, camping, picnicking, historic district tours, wildlife viewing, birding, nature photography, star gazing, and horseback riding, miles of trails are open to horses and permitted stock (burros, mules, hoofed mammals).

« Travel is the only thing you buy that makes you richer. »
- Anonymous

DATE(S) VISITED:

WEATHER:

☐ ☐ ☐ ☐ ☐

SEASON:

☐ ☐ ☐ ☐

COMPANIONS: _____

_____

_____

_____

SPECIAL MEMORIES: _____

_____

_____

_____

_____

_____

_____

_____

_____

_____

SIGHTS: _____

_____

_____

_____

_____

_____

_____

_____

NOTES:

_____

_____

_____

_____

_____

_____

_____

_____

_____

_____

PHOTOS, STAMPS:

RATING: / 10   **WILL RETURN?** YES / NO

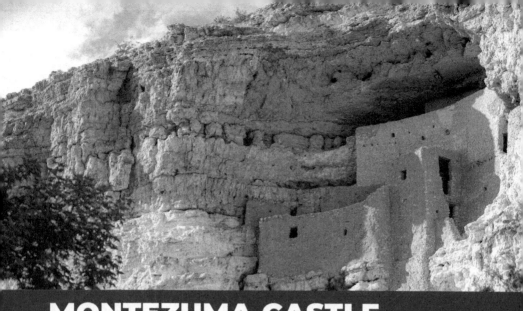

MONTEZUMA CASTLE
34.6116° N, 111.8350° W

Today, approximately 350,000 people per year visit the Castle, browse the museum, and stroll through the scenic sycamore grove. The towering trees offer welcome shade and critical habitat for hundreds of native plants and animals. Montezuma Castle, comprising 840 acres, is located approximately within the town of Camp Verde, it's about 45 minutes (50 miles) south of Flagstaff and an hour (90 miles) north of Phoenix, Arizona. It can be reached by taking Exit 289 off I-17 and following the signs 3 miles to the Visitor Center parking lot. Montezuma's Castle is definitely one of the best things to do in Arizona because it's such a unique "castle." This limestone cliff dwelling is of the Sinagua culture from about 800 years ago. It is 20 rooms tall and until the 1950s visitors could climb up to it via ladders. The scale of this place is insane. It definitely makes you think about the craftsmanship and ingenuity of the architecture. There are a few trails around the area and guided tours, plus great signage to read about the history.

BEST TIMES TO VISIT:
The best time to visit Montezuma Castle National Monument is in February, followed by January and March.

A QUICK GUIDE TO VISITING MONTEZUMA CASTLE N. MONUMENT:
The Montezuma Castle Monument actually contains 16 district structures, of which the site named Montezuma Castle is just one. The structures were built around 1125 AD during the Honaki phase of the Sinagua culture. The Sinagua people occupied this site until roughly 1425 AD, when they abandoned the land during the Tuzigoot phase of the culture. The Montezuma Castle is a five-story, stone structure situated 50 feet above the valley of the river Verde. The structure makes use of available materials

ich as limestone blocks, mud plaster, and soil mortar. The architectural features f the castle showcase both regular rectangular doorways as well as more stylistic -shaped doorways, which are reflective of the dominant style during the era in which was built. It also features windows, vents near the floor, and ceiling hatchways. The rnamental details discovered in the structure include viga and latlilla ceilings as well s numerous fireplaces. In addition to the Montezuma Castle, visitors can view the tructure referred to as Castle A, a large limestone cliff dwelling used by the Sinagua eople. This site was originally excavated by Earl Jackson in 1933. The excavation nd subsequent testing revealed that in its heyday, Castle A was much bigger than he Montezuma Castle, containing at least five floors and 45 rooms. Of these, only 26 emain due to the fact that much of the front section of the 5th, 4th, and 3rd floors ad fallen off. Many of the same design features noted in the Montezuma Castle are eplicated in Castle A, including the use of vigas and latillas, limestone blocks, and ud mortar. The hearths and the storage spaces carved into the cave walls humanize he structure, providing an inside look into the ways in which the Sinagua were able o survive and even thrive in the harsh desert climate.

'isitors seeking shelter from the unrelenting desert sun can find it among the shaded orest located on the outer rim of Montezuma Castle Well. There are sycamore trees,

esert flowers, birds, and many species of mammals from a unique ecosystem, which isitors can experience first-hand. Budding botanists will be interested to know that ycamore trees, aside from providing natural shade groves, were utilized by the inagua for their medicinal benefits. For the Sinagua people of antiquity, the well vas a life-giving resource at the center of community life. Even today, over 1.5 million rallons of water find their way into the well from the Verde River. The water enters he well through a swallet and exits through an irrigation ditch built over 1,000 years go. To this day, many residents of Rimrock, Arizona, utilize these irrigation ditches o provide water for their livestock and gardens.

« The journey is my home. »
- Muriel Rukeyser

DATE(S) VISITED:

WEATHER:

☀ ☁ ⛅ 🌧 🌫

☐ ☐ ☐ ☐ ☐

SEASON:

❄ 🌱 ☀ 🌧

☐ ☐ ☐ ☐

COMPANIONS:

_____

_____

_____

_____

SPECIAL MEMORIES:

_____

_____

_____

_____

_____

_____

_____

_____

_____

_____

SIGHTS:

_____

_____

_____

_____

_____

_____

_____

_____

_____

NOTES:

_____
_____
_____
_____
_____
_____
_____
_____
_____

PHOTOS, STAMPS:

RATING: ___ / 10   **WILL RETURN?**   YES / NO

VERMILION CLIFFS
36.8625° N, 111.8270° W

Like many people, much of our exposure to the desert southwest has come through photos. And no place has been so visually captivating as visiting the Vermilion Cliffs National Monument, which includes the areas known as Coyote Buttes, The Wave, and White Pocket. Hiking is the most popular activity, but visitors to the area also enjoy camping, photography, and wildlife viewing. This 280,000-acre monument bumps up against the Utah/Arizona border, where the wooded Paria Plateau stretches south, dropping 3,000 feet at the monument's namesake—the Vermilion Cliffs. Paria Canyon, a sinuous slot canyon along the Paria River, cuts across the northeast corner of the monument and offers a true wilderness experience for those who want to explore. Most people visiting the monument today come to see The Wave, Buckskin Gulch, and Paria Canyon, which are all located in the northwest part of the monument generally called Coyote Buttes. These incredibly scenic features, with their vibrant colors and intriguing forms, attract photographers, artists, and tourists alike.

BEST TIMES TO VISIT:
The best times to visit are typically April, May, September, and October.

A QUICK GUIDE TO VISITING VERMILION CLIFFS N. MONUMENT:
House Rock Valley Road (BLM 1065) is the main access route in the monument that connects to other dirt roads and trailheads. From Kanab, Utah, head east on Hwy 89 towards Page, Arizona, or head south on Hwy 89A through Jacob Lake—House Rock Valley Road runs north/south between these two highways. Roads in the monument are unpaved, often washboarded or filled with deep sand, and may require 4WD depending on conditions.

The Best Hikes and Trails are:

Coyote Buttes North (The Wave): This strenuous, 6.4-mile roundtrip hike begins at a riverbed and crosses challenging terrain. There's no clearly marked trail or directional markers, so you'll need a map and compass to find your way. Once you get to The Wave, you can continue to a nearby second wave formation, petroglyphs, natural arches, and dinosaur tracks.

Paria Canyon: Hikers follow the Paria River, walking on trails alongside it or through the water itself. Even using the trails, you'll get wet. You can go as far as you want; experienced backpackers will even make a 5-day trip of it. Permits obtained through a lottery are required for an overnight stay.

Coyote Buttes South: There are no marked trails in this area, so you'll need excellent navigation skills to make your way. You'll also want a high-clearance, four-wheel-drive vehicle since the roads leading into this permitted area cut through deep sand. Every year, inexperienced, unprepared drivers get stranded on these roads. Don't be one of them.

White Pocket: There are no marked trails to these whitish-grey sandstone formations, so once again, you'll need strong wayfinding skills to get to them. And a high-clearance, four-wheel-drive vehicle.

Buckskin Gulch: A 20-mile hike best completed over a period of several days, this trail navigates through the longest and deepest slot canyon in the Southwest. Be prepared for obstacles, including rocks, pools, escapable quicksand, and possible flash floods.

« To travel is to live. »
- Hans Christian Anderson

DATE(S) VISITED:

WEATHER:

☐ ☐ ☐ ☐ ☐

SEASON:

☐ ☐ ☐ ☐

COMPANIONS: _____

_____
_____
_____

SPECIAL MEMORIES: _____

_____
_____
_____
_____
_____
_____
_____
_____
_____
_____

SIGHTS: _____

_____
_____
_____
_____
_____
_____
_____
_____
_____

NOTES: _____

PHOTOS, STAMPS:

RATING: / 10   WILL RETURN?   YES / NO

WUPATKI
35.5600° N, 111.3935° W

Established in 1924, the Wupatki National Monument – part of a collective of Flagstaff Area National Monuments, including Sunset Crater Volcano and Walnut Canyon – is a nature and culture preserve. Ancient peoples once inhabited the area, leaving behind their pueblos, or villages, when they moved on. Today, travelers can hike through the park's red rocks, pausing at the village ruins along the way and learning about the day-to-day lives of the people who once called Wupatki home.

BEST TIMES TO VISIT:
The area welcomes visitors in all seasons. But the best times to visit are typically April, May, September, and October.

A QUICK GUIDE TO VISITING WUPATKI NATIONAL MONUMENT:
Most trails in the park are at least partially accessible. The main trail, Wupatki Pueblo Trail, is accessible to an overlook approximately 200 feet from the visitor center where it begins. Similarly, the Citadel and Nalakihu Pueblos Trail is accessible past both pueblos, ending at the base of a cinder hill, while Wukoki Pueblo Trail is accessible to the pueblo. Only the Lomaki and Box Canyon Pueblos Trail is inaccessible. Additionally, the Wupatki Visitor Center is accessible. In addition to the restrooms, ramps, and automatic entry and exit doors, the visitor center features a film with closed captioning and Braille and large text versions of the park brochure.

All activity starts at the park's visitor center, where you can learn about the Ancient Puebloans and see artifacts. Kids can also pick up Junior Ranger activities there. Behind the visitor center, the Wupatki Pueblo Trail leads to the park's main ruins, the largest free-standing pueblo in northern Arizona. Nearby, the Wukoki Pueblo stands three stories tall and overlooks the desert all the way to the San Francisco Peaks. The remaining four pueblos are several miles down the road. Citadel and Nalakihu pueblos appear to be single-family dwellings while the Lomaki and Box Canyon pueblos feature limestone and sandstone construction.

The Best Hikes and Trails are:

Crack-in-Rock: Available on certain weekends in October and April, this guided, 18- to 20-mile roundtrip hike follows an unmarked route and requires hikers to overnight in the backcountry. Reservations are required, and there is a fee. Expect extreme temperatures, wind, and challenging terrain. You'll also have to carry a minimum gallon of water per day plus your backpack.

Nukoki Pueblo Trail: This 0.2-mile trail goes to a pueblo built on a sandstone outcrop. Accessible up to the base of the trail, it takes about 15 minutes to explore.

Discovery Hikes: Offered some Saturdays October through April, these ranger-led hikes leave the visitor center at noon and visit backcountry pueblos otherwise off-limits to the general public. Reservations are required, and the group size is limited to 12 people. All three hikes—Kaibab House, Antelope House, and East Mesa—are moderately strenuous and take about three hours to complete.

Wupatki Pueblo Trail: The most popular trail in the park, this 0.5-mile walk loops

around a 104-room pueblo with a ball court and blowhole. It is accessible to the scenic overlook. Plan to spend up to an hour on this trail.

Where to Camp: Camping is available throughout Coconino National Forest, which is very close to Wupatki National Monument. However, some of the forest service campgrounds close during the winter. Confirm the campground you plan to stay at is open before you head out. If it is closed, the Flagstaff KOA is open year-round.

Bonito Campground: Adjacent to Sunset Crater Volcano National Monument, this seasonal forest service campground features picnic tables, grills, fire rings, flush toilets, and drinking water.

Flagstaff KOA: Has 200 campsites available plus tents and cabins.

« Travel – the best way to be lost and found at the same time. »
- Brenna Smith

DATE(S) VISITED:

WEATHER:

☐ ☐ ☐ ☐ ☐

SEASON:

☐ ☐ ☐ ☐

COMPANIONS:

SPECIAL MEMORIES:

SIGHTS:

NOTES:

_____
_____
_____
_____
_____
_____
_____
_____
_____
_____

PHOTOS, STAMPS:

RATING: / 10   **WILL RETURN?** YES / NO

TONTO NATURAL BRIDGE
34.3229° N, 111.4544° W

Tonto Natural Bridge State Park is something everyone should experience at least once in their lifetime. If you're passing through the area, it's well worth just pulling over to marvel at this incredible natural wonder in Tonto Natural Bridge State Park. However, if you have the time, we highly recommend spending at least a day enjoying everything that Tonto Natural Bridge State Park has to offer. This state park is in Pine Creek Canyon just north of Payson, AZ, and is surrounded by tree-covered mountains. Tonto Natural Bridge is known to be the world's largest natural travertine bridge, standing 183-feet high over a 400-foot-long tunnel that measures 150 feet at its widest point. It's one of the most beautiful natural bridges in the United States, and unique in that most natural bridges are made of sandstone or limestone, not travertine. Be sure to stop by the visitor center, which has some cool history about the area, as well as park information.

BEST TIMES TO VISIT:
Although you can visit year-round, you'll experience the best weather during the spring and fall. The winters can get below freezing, and the average temperature is around 90 degrees in the summer months. you should note that the last possible park entry is 4:00 p.m. Anna Mae, Gowan, Pine Creek, and Waterfall Trails close at 4:00 p.m. The paved path and all viewpoints remain open until 5:00 p.m.

A QUICK GUIDE TO VISITING TONTO NATURAL BRIDGE STATE PARK:
Tonto Natural Bridge State Park is about halfway between Phoenix and Flagstaff, roughly two hours away from either city by car. Interstate 17 is the highway that connects the two cities and you have to turn off onto Highway 260 heading east for about an hour until you reach the entrance for the state park.

and on top of the bridge at any of the four observation points and explore the travertine rocks in the 400-foot tunnel running through the bridge's center. The park also offers four hiking trails, which descend into the Pine Canyon and capture the magnificence of this geologic wonder. Picnic areas are available throughout the park, so don't forget to pack lunch to enjoy under the trees. There are some small waterfalls around the natural bridge with pools of water, but visitors are not allowed to swim in the area directly around the bridge. However, you can walk along Pine Creek and swim further downstream, which is especially refreshing on a hot summer day in Arizona. The Goodfellow Lodge is the park's visitor's center, including a small museum with exhibits about the history of the park, how travertine is made, and the indigenous residents of central Arizona.

The Best Hikes and Trails: There are only four trails within the state park and the longest one is only a half-mile. However, even the shortest trails that are only a few hundred feet involve steep descents, uneven stairs, and sometimes climbing over slippery rocks. Make sure you have the right footwear before starting any of the hikes and factor in more time than you think you'll need for the whole trip.

Pine Creek Trail: This trail is about a half-mile long and goes down to the water at the bottom of the tunnel. The first 400 feet is on a paved path but the rest of it is on rocks,

some of which can be slippery from the creek.

Waterfall Trail: This trail is about 300 feet long and ends at a waterfall cave. It should take less than a half-hour but note that there are uneven steps.

Anna Mae Trail: Only about 500 feet long, This short and sweet trail leads to Pine Creek Trail and the Natural Bridge.

Gowan Trail: This half-mile trail is steep and strenuous, but it takes trekkers to an observation deck at the bottom of the creek to get a full view of the tunnel. It takes about an hour to complete the roundtrip journey.

* Note: Dogs are allowed at the viewpoints and parking area but they are not permitted on any of the trails.

« Travel teaches toleration. »
- Benjamin Disraeli

DATE(S) VISITED:

WEATHER:

☐ ☐ ☐ ☐ ☐

SEASON:

☐ ☐ ☐ ☐

COMPANIONS:

SPECIAL MEMORIES:

SIGHTS:

NOTES:

_____

_____

_____

_____

_____

_____

_____

_____

_____

_____

PHOTOS, STAMPS:

RATING: / 10   WILL RETURN?   YES / NO

ANTELOPE CANYON
36.8619° N, 111.3743° W

According to local legend, Antelope Canyon was discovered by a young girl while tending her sheep. Regardless of how and when it was discovered, it is no doubt one of the most beautiful natural wonders in the United States. Formed by water over millions of years, reddish-brown Navajo sandstone gracefully bends and curves as it stretches through one and a half miles of slot canyons just outside of Page, Arizona. Opened to the public in 1997, Antelope Canyon has become one of the most popular attractions in northern Arizona, attracting over one million visitors a year. And for photographers, it's become a bucket list destination. Supposedly, professional photographer Peter Lik sold a photo of Antelope Canyon for $6.5 million. And while that story can't be verified, it underscores the popularity of this otherworldly site and the thousands of ways it can be captured by the camera.

BEST TIMES TO VISIT:
The best time to visit Antelope Canyon is between the end of March and the beginning of October. In terms of the best time of day to visit the canyon, going between 11 am and 1:30 pm will give you the highest chance of seeing Antelope Canyon light beams in the Upper section of Antelope Canyon.

A QUICK GUIDE TO VISITING TONTO NATURAL BRIDGE STATE PARK:
Located on Navajo Nation land, Antelope Canyon is east of Page, Arizona, just a bit south of the Utah border. The closest international airports are Las Vegas McCarran International or Phoenix Sky Harbor in Arizona — each about a 4 and 1-half hour drive to Page. Public transportation is limited in the area, so it's recommended to have your own car or rent one at the airport.

pper Antelope Canyon is the most accessible part of Antelope Canyon. It has no airs or ladders. It is also only a short walk, making it ideal for those with very young ildren or anybody with mobility issues. This tour has become extremely popular d often sells out months in advance. You are best to make advance reservations as on as you know what dates you will be in the area.

wer Antelope Canyon is an excellent section of the canyon. The tours travel in e direction, making it slightly easier to get photographs of the canyon with fewer eople in it. It has some dramatic stairs, ladders, and narrow sections. This makes r some great shots, but be aware that everybody in your party needs to be able to mfortably climb a steep stairwell. With multiple departures a day, your tour will last out 1.5-2 hours and your guide will tell you about the history of the canyon, point ut particular points of interest, and make sure your experience is enjoyable, fun, and fe. You can tour this canyon as a stand-alone tour, or you can combine it with the ntelope Canyon Boat tour, or see both upper and lower canyon to get the most out f your visit.

ake Powell has been a regional attraction for decades but has only recently seen enewed interest with the rapid growth of Antelope Canyon. As Antelope Canyon

idens as it approaches Lake Powell, it eventually turns into a side canyon with oat access. While Antelope Point Marina is worthy of a visit itself, the highlight r the curious visitor is the boat tour that brings you up Antelope Canyon from the aterside. Most tours take about an hour, and you will experience Antelope Canyon om a completely different perspective, while also getting a taste of the soaring cliffs f Lake Powell.

« *A good traveler has no fixed plans, and is not intent on arriving.* »
- *Lao Tzu*

DATE(S) VISITED:

WEATHER:

☐ ☐ ☐ ☐ ☐

SEASON:

☐ ☐ ☐ ☐

COMPANIONS:

SPECIAL MEMORIES:

SIGHTS:

NOTES:

_____
_____
_____
_____
_____
_____
_____
_____
_____
_____

PHOTOS, STAMPS:

RATING: / 10   WILL RETURN?   YES / NO

CATALINA
32.4364° N, 110.9096° W

Flanking the northern edge of the Catalina Foothills district, Catalina State Park provides spectacular views of Tucson and the surrounding mountain ranges. Inside, the park hosts 5,500 acres of canyons, streams, and hiking and biking trails that wind through the Coronado National Forest at elevations near 3,000 feet. Along with the gorgeous views. Some visitors choose to hike, but you can also explore the park trails on horseback. Sitting at the eastern edge of the park, Houston's Horseback Riding offers guided trail rides. Recent visitors called the park a "feast for the eyes" and said the high bird population is "astounding." Thanks to its location about 40 miles north of downtown Tucson, the park makes for an easy day trip, according to reviewers.

BEST TIMES TO VISIT:
The best times to visit are from April to May and from September to October.

A QUICK GUIDE TO VISITING CATALINA STATE PARK:
The central core of the Catalina Mountains is granite of Laramide origin, altered by metamorphism to gneiss along its western side. Catalina State Park is located near the base of the fore range anticline, which drains into Cañon de Oro to the west. The parkland is situated on sedimentary Miocene (25 million-year-old) deposits of sandstone, limestone, mudstone, and conglomerates.

Plants within Catalina State Park lie within the Lower Sonoran Life zone. They include mesquite, paloverde, and acacia trees; crucfixuion thorn, ocotillo, cholla, prickly pear, and Saguaro Cactus. Desert Willow, Arizona Sycamore, Arizona Ash, and native walnut grow along the washes. Jack and cottontail rabbits, Mule Deer, Javelina, Coyotes, ground squirrels, packrats, and numerous lizards and snakes live ithin the park. More than 150 species of birds call the park home. Mountain Lions, ighorn Sheep, and Black Bears have also been observed on rare occasions.

he Best Hikes and Trails are:

omero Ruins Interpretive Trail: This is a hiking-only trail, which is under 1 mile. The asy loop starts at the main parking lot (near the picnic area) and features signs that xplain the history and culture of the Hohokom village. Note that this trail crosses a ash so water may be present after rainfall.

ature Trail: A great option for kids, Catalina State Park's Nature Trail is a 1-mile loop r hikers and bicyclists to enjoy.

irding Trail (1.4 mi): is the only completely flat trail in the park, connecting the questrian Center with the main trailhead.

ridle Trail: This flat 1.4-mile trail, which is often used by horseback riders, connects e Equestrian Center and the trailhead.

anyon Loop Trail: Beginning at the park trailhead, this 2.3-mile loop crosses a wash everal times and takes about an hour to complete.

omero Canyon Trail: The Romero Canyon Trail (7.2 mi.) and the Sutherland Trail 0.5 mi.) offer longer, more strenuous hikes through beautiful desert terrain and parian canyons. Both climb to cool natural pools and connect with other Coronado

ational Forest trails which continue on to Mount Lemmon at the top of the Catalina lountains.

o-Year Trail: Sometimes used by daring mountain bikers, the 50-Year Trail begins at e Equestrian Center and goes for 7.8 miles. Arizona State Parks & Trails recommends nat you plan 4 hours for hiking each way.

Vhere to Camp: The Park has one of the best campgrounds in Arizona, with 120 ites complete with water and electricity. Spread out over a large area, every site has n amazing view of the mountains. The campground can accommodate RVs of any ize; even the largest will have no problem finding an ideal spot. Unique among state ampgrounds, free (and fast!) Wi-Fi is provided to patrons. Modern comfort stations, rovide hot showers and flush toilets.

« All journeys have secret destinations of which the traveler is unaware. »
- Martin Buber

DATE(S) VISITED:

WEATHER:

☐ ☐ ☐ ☐ ☐

SEASON:

☐ ☐ ☐ ☐

COMPANIONS: _____
_____
_____
_____

SPECIAL MEMORIES: _____
_____
_____
_____
_____
_____
_____
_____
_____
_____

SIGHTS: _____
_____
_____
_____
_____
_____
_____
_____
_____
_____

NOTES:

_____

_____

_____

_____

_____

_____

_____

_____

_____

_____

PHOTOS, STAMPS:

RATING: / 10   WILL RETURN?   YES / NO

SLIDE ROCK
34.9436° N, 111.7529° W

Slide Rock State Park features a natural rock water slide located in Oak Creek Canyon just 15 minutes from Sedona and 40 minutes from Flagstaff. Slide Rock State Park was originally the Pendley Homestead but today is known as one of "America's Top 10 Swimming Holes". But the crisp creek water is not the only draw to the area. Slide Rock State Park is surrounded by famous red rocks and desert scenery. So beautiful in fact, that many movies including "Angel and the Badman" (1946) with John Wayne were filmed there. The historic apple orchard in Oak Creek Canyon which is also home to Slide Rock was originally the pioneering property of Frank L. Pendley.

BEST TIMES TO VISIT:
Summer and fall bring the bulk of area tourism because the weather is nearly perfect for all kinds of outdoor adventures.

BEST THINGS TO DO IN SLIDE ROCK STATE PARK:
1. Oak Creek Red Rock Water Slide: The cool to cold waters of Oak Creek ensure the constant flow of water down the chute. Algae growth on the rocks gives it a slippery effect that makes for an even more fun ride. Sliding down the chute into a pool of waist-deep cool water is an amazing experience that provides visitors with lots of fun and excitement.

2. Oak Creek Natural Pools: Swim a few feet further downstream to reach a ledge about 6 feet above the pool from which you can even jump into the water for the experience of a bit of cliff jumping. The deeper pools are great to wade in, and the ledges are perfect spots to sunbathe, stretch out or even jump off into the pools below.

3. Orchard Canyon at Oak Creek: One mile north of the park deep in the canyon, Orchard Canyon offers a cabin set on a ten-acre site next to Oak Creek features cozy cottage-style cabins, beautiful gardens, an apple orchard, and an excellent restaurant. Orchard Canyon at Oak Creek reservations are limited and can book up months in advance.

Fishing in Oak Creek Arizona: Oak Creek features rainbow trout and if you have the necessary fishing licenses, set aside a few hours for angling at the park. Head over to the creek during fishing season to try your hand at catching one. Oak Creek is closed to fishing above Slide Rock Park, and the trout found in the creek are all small in size. Try Sedona's Rainbow Trout Farm a few miles down the road from the park for a sure catch.

The Pendley Homestead Trail: is an easy quarter-mile trail. This paved, level trail is suitable for all visitors. It travels through a portion of the historic Pendley Homestead featuring parts of the original apple orchards, the Pendley Homestead House, some tourist cabins, the apple packing barn, various farming implements that were used, a new orchard of semi-dwarf apple trees, and spectacular views.

The Slide Rock Route: is a 0.3-mile trail with a difficulty rating of moderate and is, actually, the main access to the Slide Rock swim area. It begins near the apple picking barn and you turn right to the descending steps to the creek. Then it crosses via a small footbridge. During periods of high runoff, the footbridge will not be there and visitors will just need to stay on the west side. After crossing the footbridge, you

will proceed north along pretty sandstone shelves. In the summer, sunbathers occupy much of this route.

The Clifftop Nature Trail: is a quarter-mile trail that begins near the apple barn after the steps to the creek and leads into the forest above the swim area's west side. Thus, it offers the most scenic views and is best, not only for those who want to hike but also for those who want memorable photos.

Camping: It's fun to camp out overnight when visiting Slide Rock State Park. There are three campgrounds along Oak Creek, making for a perfect overnight adventure trip. The Manzanita Campground is about half a mile south of the park, while the Cave Springs Campground is the largest in the area but a little further away. The third campground in the area is the Pine Flat campground, about a mile from the Cave Springs Campground.

« *I need a six month vacation, twice a year.* »
- Anonymous

DATE(S) VISITED:

WEATHER:

☐   ☐   ☐   ☐   ☐

SEASON:

☐   ☐   ☐   ☐

COMPANIONS:

_____

_____

_____

SPECIAL MEMORIES:

_____

_____

_____

_____

_____

_____

_____

_____

SIGHTS:

_____

_____

_____

_____

_____

_____

_____

_____

NOTES:

_____

_____

_____

_____

_____

_____

_____

_____

_____

_____

PHOTOS, STAMPS:

RATING: / 10   WILL RETURN?   YES / NO

LOST DUTCHMAN
33.4630° N, 111.4806° W

Located on the edge of the Greater Phoenix metropolitan area, Lost Dutchman State Park was founded in 1977 and has been a popular choice with Apache Junctions visitors and residents who enjoy hiking, camping, mountain biking, and other outdoor activities. The hiking trails are suitable for all levels of hikers, beginners or advanced, and can take you through the native plant garden or to the Flatiron. It's also a popular stop along the Apache Trail, one of the most scenic drives in the state. Often visitors combine an easy hike at Lost Dutchman State Park with a drive on the Apache Trail or a visit to the nearby Ghostfield Ghost Town or Superstition Mountain Museum. There are several events and programs held at the park throughout the year such as the early morning 'Salute to the Sun Hike' and going 'Desert Scorpion Hunting' in the dark of the night. Wildlife that you may come across while you're there includes javelina, jackrabbits, coyotes, and mule deer.

BEST TIMES TO VISIT:
The park's busy season is October to April when temperatures are moderate.

A QUICK GUIDE TO VISITING LOST DUTCHMAN STATE PARK:
Hiking is the most popular activity in Lost Dutchman State Park, although you can mountain bike on most of the trails as well. Start at the visitor center to learn more about the Sonoran Desert's flora and fauna before hitting the trails. You may also want to check the park's calendar as a variety of programming and events are held there, such as sunset and moonlit hikes and scorpion "hunting" with a black light.

Lost Dutchman State Park is a park that promotes earth caching. Similar to geocaching, where you use GPS to locate objects hidden by other participants, earth ching directs you to points on the trails where you can listen to interesting stories out the park or learn more about the natural landscape. Many visitors combine a op at Lost Dutchman State Park with a visit to Superstition Mountain Museum or oldfield Ghost Town, a reconstructed 1890s mining town, or the hike in the park efore continuing a drive on the scenic Apache Trail.

he Best Hikes and Trails: Lost Dutchman has everyone's hiking prowess covered.
ative Plant Trail: This .25-mile, accessible trail begins near the visitor center and atures plants native to the Sonoran Desert. Ask for the native plant trail guide at the nger station for descriptions of the plants you'll see along the way.
reasure Loop Trail: Rated moderate, this 2.4-mile, heavily-trafficked trail offers bectacular views of the Phoenix metro area as well as wildflowers from March rough early May. It has a 500-foot elevation gain.
iphon Draw Trail: For a challenge, take this 4-mile roundtrip trek through Siphon raw, a canyon that acts as a siphon, funneling water through its passage when it ins. Be careful about hiking this trail, even during light rain.
latiron: This hike follows an unmaintained route to the mountain's flat top. Allow at ast five hours to make the 5.8-mile, roundtrip journey, and be prepared to scramble.
nly physically fit, experienced hikers should attempt this hike.

Vhere to Camp: Lost Dutchman Park boasts 134 campsites housed in seven loops to ccommodate RVs, trailers, and tents. Open all year round, the campground consists f dry campsites, 68 electric hookup sites, and overflow sites. Some of the amenities vailable in Lost Dutchman State Park Campground include a dump station and vo shower and restroom buildings, so you will be able to enjoy some luxuries. Each ampsite is also equipped with a picnic table, fire ring, and a grill, so if you want to ook up a storm, you will be able to without having to leave your campsite. Trailers nd RVs up to 140 feet in length can be accommodated. The cell signal is fairly good, ut there is no Wi-Fi connectivity. Generator use is allowed from 8.00 AM to 9.00 PM. you want to enjoy your RV vacation without distraction, remember to bring noise-anceling headphones with you.

« Tourists don't know where they've been, travelers don't know where they're going. »
- Paul Theroux

DATE(S) VISITED:

WEATHER:

☐ ☐ ☐ ☐ ☐

SEASON:

☐ ☐ ☐ ☐

COMPANIONS: _____

_____

_____

_____

SPECIAL MEMORIES: _____

_____

_____

_____

_____

_____

_____

_____

_____

_____

SIGHTS: _____

_____

_____

_____

_____

_____

_____

_____

_____

_____

NOTES:

_____

_____

_____

_____

_____

_____

_____

_____

_____

_____

PHOTOS, STAMPS:

RATING: / 10   WILL RETURN?   YES / NO

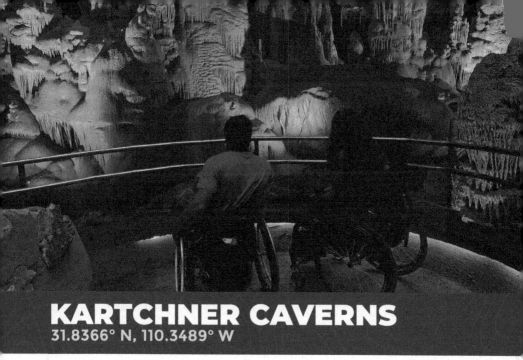

KARTCHNER CAVERNS
31.8366° N, 110.3489° W

Arizona is a wondrous state for its diverse, natural, and awe-inspiring beauty. Everyone is familiar with the state's most popular tourist sights. However, there's one sight that may not be familiar to you: A state park located about an hour south of Tucson. Kartchner Caverns. Boasting the world's longest stalactite formation. Discovered in 1974, Kartchner Caverns is a massive limestone cave that's home to many outstanding features, including remarkable minerals and formations as well as some winged friends. Kartchner Caverns Located in Southern Arizona, this ADA-accessible park is just a short hop from Tucson in nearby Benson.

BEST TIMES TO VISIT:
Mid-October to mid-April, when both cave tours are available. The Big Room Tour shuts down during summer so as not to disturb the nesting bat population.

A QUICK GUIDE TO VISITING KARTCHNER CAVERNS STATE PARK:
The 23,000-square-foot Discovery Center features a multi-screen video that tells the history of the cave and gives the explorer's perspective of cave preservation. From the visitor center to the cave's entrance, you will ride in an electric tram. The rest of the trip is walking on concrete walkways. In the cave, rangers will lead the tour on 40" wide walkways with handrails. The paths wind through two major chambers in the cave, the Rotunda and Throne rooms. Each cave tour is guided by a State Park Ranger. The tour is about 1/2 mile long underground and encompasses two big football-field-sized rooms called the Rotunda and Throne rooms and an exquisite passage called the Imaginary room. Because this is an environmental cave, it has been protected to educate and teach "cave ethics." Arizona State Parks does not encourage exploring caves but rather experiencing the beauty of the natural, pristine setting that has been

otected. Visitors may see native animals, such as deer, in the park. Inside the cave, owever, most of the animal life is confined to the "Big Room" portion of the cave. The ats are only in the "Big Room" during the summer months and must not be disturbed their maternity nursery. Both sound and light may affect the 1,000 Myotis velifer ats from coming back to the cave each year. An exhibit in the Discovery Center escribes the maternity roosting area and the habits of the bats. Marvel at the many range and colorful formations. Learn about the cave fauna, both living and ancient. xperience the wonder of the cave's discovery and learn about new scientific research nd discoveries as ongoing studies continue.

n addition to the cave tour, a variety of recreational opportunities are available to sitors at Kartchner Caverns. Hiking in the Whetstone Mountains above the cave ill be popular. Picnicking, walking on the Humming garden around the Discovery enter, and eating under the ramada area additional day-use activities.

iking: Kartchner Caverns State Park has one of the most beautiful biking trails ou've ever pedaled. While many of the trails are shared and non-motorized, the one at stands out for biking is the Guindani Trail. The trailhead is on the west end of the ain access road, at the Upper Volunteer Village. The trail winds its way out of park oundaries, through the Whetstone Mountains, and into Coronado National Forest.

Make sure to carry sufficient water with you as this beautiful trail is in the desert.

est Hikes & Trails: Kartchner Caverns State Park has plenty of trails to explore. rom the two-mile Foothills Loop Trail, you can make your way to the scenic Mountain iewpoint, or branch out for a more challenging hike on the 4.2-mile Guindani Trail. Or if you want a peaceful walk without running into any cyclers or motorized vehicles, ike the foot-traffic-only Ocotillo Trail, which covers roughly 3.2 miles of beautiful esert terrain. In addition, there are trails connecting the parking area to different ections of the campground if you just want to get off the beaten path for a walkabout.

amping: With 62 campsites, big rig access, tent camping, cabins, and more, Kartch- er Caverns State Park provides a variety of accommodations. RV campers will ap- reciate well-paved, flat roads, broad sweeping turns, and ample parking. A relatively mall campground area provides a tight-knit community feel.

« Adventure is worthwhile. »
- Aesop

DATE(S) VISITED:

WEATHER: SEASON:

☐   ☐   ☐   ☐   ☐   ☐   ☐   ☐   ☐

COMPANIONS:

_____
_____
_____

SPECIAL MEMORIES:

_____
_____
_____
_____
_____
_____
_____
_____
_____

SIGHTS:

_____
_____
_____
_____
_____
_____
_____
_____
_____

NOTES:

_____

_____

_____

_____

_____

_____

_____

_____

_____

_____

PHOTOS, STAMPS:

RATING: / 10   WILL RETURN?   YES / NO

DEAD HORSE RANCH
34.7537° N, 112.0216° W

The developed portion of Dead Horse Ranch State Park covers 423 acres. The 3,300 foot elevation accounts for the mild temperatures ideal for mountain biking in the Coconino National Forest, canoeing, picnicking, fishing, or wading in the cool water. Dead Horse is also adjacent to the Verde River Greenway State Natural Area, which conserves land in its natural state. If you're eager to experience Arizona's nature in its purest form, this is the place to be. A unique ecosystem and riparian zone offer plenty of opportunity to enjoy the outdoors. And you'll want to make more than one trip, too – life along the river changes with the seasons so there's always something new to experience. More than 300 birds fly through the park each year—from predatory falcons and migrating species to the inquisitive cactus wren, the state bird of Arizona. On a bench in a clearing, shaded by cottonwoods and studded with bird feeders, it is easy to spot at least 15 different types of birds in less than two hours. On the trails birders regularly identify dozens of species on any given day. The 423-acre park is an oasis for wildlife because it is located in the heart of Verde River's lush riparian corridor, along the banks of the free-flowing Verde River. Only a few minutes from Cottonwood's busy Main Street.

BEST TIMES TO VISIT:
The best times to visit Dead Horse Ranch State Park in the fall season.

A QUICK GUIDE TO VISITING DEAD HORSE RANCH STATE PARK:
Fishing in the river or 4-acre lagoon that are both periodically stocked with trout, sunfish, and catfish to the delight of anglers and a resident population of Great Blue Herons. Picnicking is available in one of two armadas or by the lagoon, Grilling in the armadas or campsites, and Learning about the wildlife and attractions in the area.

Where to Camp: Dead Horse Ranch has five campground loops. The Upper Campgrounds (Red-Tail Hawk Loop, Cooper's Hawk Loop, and Blackhawk Loop) have a combined 127 campsites while the Lower Campgrounds (Quail Loop and Raven Loop) have a combined 68 campsites. Most campsites are RV accessible with hookups, and many of the pull-through sites can accommodate trailers up to 65 feet long. While the campgrounds are all just a few minutes from the lagoons and the Verde River, none of the campsites are on the water. Quail Loop is the closest campground to the lagoons and river.

Note: Reservations are encouraged since campsites fill up, especially on weekends.

The Best Hikes and Trails are:

Mesa: This 1-mile interpretative trail circles the hilltop west of Red-Tail Hawk Campground. Offshoots continue south, parallel to Roadrunner Road, all the way to Dead Horse Ranch Road.

Canopy: Located south of the ranger station, near the River Day Use Area, this quarter-mile, ADA-accessible loop takes its name from the Fremont tree canopy overhead. Keep an eye out for birds and other wildlife.

Lagoon trails: An accessible loop circles each of the park's three lagoons. Expect to walk approximately 0.4 miles each around West and Middle lagoons and 0.72 miles around East Lagoon. Bicycles are permitted, but horses are discouraged.

Verde River Greenway: This 2-mile trail follows the Verde River, passing through some of the best areas in the park for bird watching. Pick up the trail in the River Day Use Area or near one of the lagoon trails.

Lime Kiln: Completed in 2006, this 15-mile, shared-use trail follows a portion of the historic Lime Kiln Wagon Road and connects Dead Horse Ranch to Red Rock State Park.

« Once a year, go someplace you've never been before. »
- Dalai Lama

DATE(S) VISITED:

WEATHER:

☐ ☐ ☐ ☐ ☐

SEASON:

☐ ☐ ☐ ☐

COMPANIONS:

SPECIAL MEMORIES:

SIGHTS:

NOTES:

PHOTOS, STAMPS:

RATING: / 10 WILL RETURN? YES / NO

LAKES
WATERFALLS
HIKES

Arizona is a diverse state with an arid desert, towering mountains, and lush landscapes around Flagstaff. It's hard to pick the very best lakes, waterfalls, and hikes in Arizona when the state is home to a lot of them.

There's something therapeutic about standing at the base of a waterfall or in a pure lake. Even hiking a new path, add at least one of these unique attractions to your itinerary for a true Arizona experience!

PLAN IT | DO IT | JOURNAL IT

LAKE HAVASU
34.4839° N, 114.3225° W

Established in 1965, this state park offers 928 acres of outdoor recreation and fu
Lake Havasu State Park is located on the shores of Lake Havasu and features clea
white sand beaches and a large grassy area. The park offers panoramic views of th
lake and mountains beyond. Lake Havasu State Park is the place to go campin
swimming, fishing, hiking, and more in a sunny and beautiful Arizona nature settin
The park is open to the public all year round, 24 hours a day, with outdoor trails ar
beachside campsites for tents or RVs, tucked right up against the gorgeous Colorac
River.

BEST TIMES TO VISIT:
Fall, winter, and spring are ideal times to hike park trails to view wildlife, birds, ar
other Colorado River beauty. A Lake Havasu winter will typically show you warm day
and cool nights.. perfect to enjoy a campfire in the campgrounds or within the cabi
area!

A QUICK GUIDE TO VISITING LAKE HAVASU STATE PARK:
Campsites are equipped with power for RVs and have easy access to restrooms, fi
rings, picnic tables, and potable drinking water. The park is a popular port of entry fc
boats on the river and offers canoe and kayak rental to visitors looking for a day c
the water as well as maps and guides for guests looking to explore the trails. Picn
tables, grills, and shade covers make this the perfect site to spend the day on th
beach; or you may want to stay and camp awhile. There are also group picnic area
for a family reunion or other special occasions.

For those who enjoy hiking and walking, the park has the Mohave Sunset Trail, a short but scenic 1.75-mile walk, and the Arroyo-Camino Interpretive Garden, home to diverse species of plants and wildlife. Birdwatchers may spot Anna's Hummingbird or a Great Horned Owl. Lake Havasu State Park is a favorite launch spot for boaters. Five boat ramps are available to all watercraft users; non-motorized watercraft may launch at any ramp. The beach area is also accessible by boat, with courtesy docks available for drop-off and pick-up (15-minute mooring).

One of the most popular things to do in Lake Havasu City attends the myriad of events that occur throughout the year. Some of the major events that take place at Lake Havasu State Park include the Havasu Balloon Festival & Fair, the Lake Havasu Boat Show, and more.

Arizona's state parks provide perfect destinations for family camping adventures without the need for an RV or tent. These new cabins at Lake Havasu State Park offer a comfortable stay in the heart of this popular and scenic outdoor destination. You can make cabin reservations up to a year in advance. For reservations, visit AZStateParks.com. The 13 new camping cabins are located with the best views in the park, right on the shore of the Colorado River. Each cabin has space to sleep up to six people and

features a queen bed with a mattress and two pairs of bunk beds with mattresses. Campers supply their own linens or sleeping bags.

Amenities include a fire ring, barbecue, and picnic tables, ramada, and adjacent white sand beach. Although these are dry cabins, brand-new restroom facilities are located just steps away. Plus, solar electricity, heating, and air conditioning make your stay comfortable any time of year.

* Note: Camping facilities at the park include 47 tent and RV sites with 50 amp electric hookups and potable water at all sites. Restrooms, showers, picnic areas, dump station and on-site boat ramp use are included in camping fees.

« *Life begins at the end of your comfort zone.* »
- Neale Donald Walsch

DATE(S) VISITED:

WEATHER:

☐ ☐ ☐ ☐ ☐

SEASON:

☐ ☐ ☐ ☐

COMPANIONS: _____

_____

_____

_____

SPECIAL MEMORIES: _____

_____

_____

_____

_____

_____

_____

_____

_____

SIGHTS: _____

_____

_____

_____

_____

_____

_____

_____

_____

NOTES: _____

_____

_____

_____

_____

_____

_____

_____

_____

_____

_____

PHOTOS, STAMPS:

RATING: / 10   WILL RETURN?   YES / NO

LAKE MEAD
36.1435° N, 114.4144° W

Interestingly, Lake Mead is the largest manmade reservoir in the United State spanning over 110 miles long in Nevada and Arizona. When Lake Mead is at its fulles it boasts 759 miles of shoreline, is 532 feet deep, has 247 square miles of surface, and a astounding 28 million-acre feet of water. The lake was formed when the United State Bureau of Reclamation selected the narrow Black Canyon section of the Colorac River for the site of what would later be called Hoover Dam.

BEST TIMES TO VISIT:
The fall season of October and November are said to be the best months to vis Lake Mead. Summer heat is now gone and the cooler fall season is setting in. Winc are generally light and comfortable. Daytime high air temperatures range from 72-9 degrees.

A QUICK GUIDE TO VISITING LAKE MEAD:
Lake Mead, Nevada is located on the Colorado River, about 25 miles from the La Vegas Strip, southeast of Las Vegas, in the states of both Nevada and Arizona. Th Lake Mead Reservoir provides water to Arizona, California, Nevada, and parts (Mexico, where farmlands and nearly 20 million benefit from its sustenance.

Originally named after Elwood Mead, the commissioner for the U.S. Bureau (Reclamation, Boulder Dam Recreation Area was established in 1936 and administere by the National Park Service. The name was changed to Lake Mead Nation: Recreation Area in 1964 when Lake Mohave and Shivwits Plateau were added.

While Lake Mead has not reached full capacity in quite some time (1983 to be exact), as of fall 2017, it is at approximately 40% with about 10 million-acre feet of held water. Both Lake Mead and the second-largest U.S. reservoir, Lake Powell, compete for capacity bragging rights. As of 2013, Lake Powell is actually in the lead!

There are nine main access points to Lake Mead, NV—on the west, three roads from the Las Vegas metropolitan area, and on the northwest, from Interstate 15 through the Valley of Fire State Park and the Moapa River Indian Reservation to the Overton Arm of the lake.

Lake Mead is broken into a number of different bodies of water. These vast bodies of water are ideal for boating and water sports, kayaking, canoeing, swimming, sunbathing, and some of the nation's best sports fishing. With 163,000 surface acres and more than 700 miles of fishable shoreline, anglers can cast their lines with the hopes of hooking several species of fish, including the striped bass, largemouth and smallmouth bass, channel catfish, bluegill, crappie, green sunfish, and rainbow trout. In most cases, all you need is a license and trout stamp to participate in this southern Nevada fishing epicenter. Additionally, the nine developed areas on the lakes offer visitors a range of accommodations and services.

If you're looking for an easy hike near Lake Mead, the Railroad Tunnel Trail is just for you. This dog-friendly hike is about 7.1 miles out and back and takes hikers up a former railroad grade. The beautiful views of Lake Mead are panoramic along this hike. You'll discover five large tunnels that were once a part of the now-gone railroad route that went from Hoover Dam and Boulder City.

« I haven't been everywhere, but it's on my list. »
- Susan Sontag

DATE(S) VISITED:

WEATHER:

☐ ☐ ☐ ☐ ☐

SEASON:

☐ ☐ ☐ ☐

COMPANIONS:

SPECIAL MEMORIES:

SIGHTS:

NOTES: _____
_____
_____
_____
_____
_____
_____
_____
_____
_____

PHOTOS, STAMPS:

RATING: / 10   WILL RETURN?   YES / NO

WATSON LAKE PARK
34.5915° N, 112.4216° W

This beautiful lake, just four miles away from downtown Prescott, features fishin
boating, kayaking, canoeing, hiking, rock climbing, camping, and day picnicking
something for everyone. Watson Lake Park is part of the Granite Dells. The del
are a unique area, with amazing Granite formations, boulders, and balanced rock
Canyons, cliffs, lakes, open fields, riparian preserves, and more are all right in front
you throughout the park. If you only have one day to spend in Prescott AZ, we hop
you include a visit to Watson Lake Park.

BEST TIMES TO VISIT:
January and February are great times to visit Watson Lake Park. The crowds are fewe
and the weather is great.

A QUICK GUIDE TO VISITING WATSON LAKE PARK:
The park is accessible from Route 89 in Prescott AZ. Coming from downtown Presco
you'll be driving North on Route 89. You'll see the Granite Dells in the distance as yo
approach from downtown. There's even a pull-off on the highway where you'll ofte
find many visitors to the area stopping in and taking pictures. We don't recommen
this area for parking. Continue North from the pull off and you'll soon reach a traff
circle that offers access to the full-day parking area at Watson Lake Park. There
a parking fee at the park, and an automated kiosk to receive a parking pass for th
day. If you plan on visiting the park often the city does offer extended passes whic
will save you a lot of money in the long run! If you're only up for a day or two, th
day passes are worth the expense. This is a rare gem to be sure. Incredible scener
where ever you look. Granite boulders stacked on top of granite rock formation
balanced rocks, and more. The beauty of this location leaves one surprised that it isr

National Forest or a National Monument. Two boat launches are available at the park. Kayaking, canoeing, fishing are all fun things to do while visiting. You will have plenty of activities to choose from during your visit, whether it is a day trip from Phoenix or a week-long camping adventure.

1. Hiking: Hiking at Watson Lake is phenomenal. The Peavine Trail runs along the southeastern side of the lake into the scenic Granite Dells region. The trail is level and easy and offers not only hiking but horseback riding and bicycling opportunities. Peavine runs into Iron King Trail for about 4 miles toward Prescott Valley. You will find lots of nooks and crannies on the trail for peaceful relaxation.

2. Mountain Biking Trails: Many of the hiking trails are also open to Mountain Bikers as well. From single-track to wide-open well-graded trails, the park offers something to all skill levels.

3. Camping at Watson Lake Park: Overnight camping is available only during the summer season. Each campsite comes with a picnic table and a fire ring with a grill. Restrooms, showers, ramadas, fish cleaning stations, a boat ramp, and a children's playground are provided.

4. Rock Climbing: The park offers excellent climbing for beginners and experienced climbers.

5. Boating: Boats with gas-powered and electric-powered motors are permitted on Watson Lake, but there is a maximum of 5 miles an hour "no wake" speed limit on the lake. Amenities include two boat launches, a courtesy dock, and fish cleaning stations.

6. Canoeing and Kayaking: Kayaks and canoes are available for rent 7 days a week (6 AM-Sunset). Rental includes kayak, paddle, dry bags & life jackets. You will love the scenery of the lake and its many hidden bays.

7. Fishing: Visitors can fish from boats or the banks of Watson Lake. State laws regarding fishing licenses apply — anyone 10 years and older must have a license to fish. The lake is popular for crappies and largemouth bass fishing.

8. Bird Watching: Watson Lake Park is an Audubon-endorsed bird watching area where you can spot hundreds of bird species, including eagles and pelicans. The 140 acres Watson Woods Riparian Preserve is located near the Peavine Trail.

« Like all great travelers, I have seen more than I remember,
and remember more than I have seen. »
- Benjamin Disraeli

DATE(S) VISITED:

WEATHER:

☐ ☐ ☐ ☐ ☐

SEASON:

☐ ☐ ☐ ☐

COMPANIONS:

_____

_____

_____

_____

SPECIAL MEMORIES:

_____

_____

_____

_____

_____

_____

_____

_____

_____

SIGHTS:

_____

_____

_____

_____

_____

_____

_____

_____

_____

NOTES: _____
_____
_____
_____
_____
_____
_____
_____
_____
_____

PHOTOS, STAMPS:

RATING: / 10   WILL RETURN?   YES / NO

FOOL HOLLOW LAKE
34.2706° N, 110.0710° W

The park along the lake, located in the Apache-Sitgreaves National Forest, opened i 1994 as a result of cooperation between the U.S. Forest Service, Arizona State Park Arizona Game and Fish, and the city of Show Low in partnership with Arizona Publ Service and McCarty Construction Company. The water surface of Fool Hollow about 150 acres with an average depth of 23 feet.

BEST TIMES TO VISIT:
The best time to visit is from March through May, the season feels moderate.

A QUICK GUIDE TO VISITING FOOL HOLLOW LAKE RECREATION AREA
Where does a name like "Fool Hollow" come from, you ask? Back in 1885, a ma by the name of Thomas Jefferson Adair settled in the area intent on farming. Th locals thought only a fool would attempt to farm that land, and the joke stuck. Foc Hollow Lake Recreation Area is located in the world's largest contiguous belt c ponderosa pine forest. A relatively flat basaltic plateau, broken by Show Low Cree and Fool Hollow Wash, characterizes the property. Fool Hollow Lake was created b the construction of a dam at the confluence of Show Low Creek and Fool Hollo Wash in 1957 by the Arizona Game and Fish Department with federal assistance. Th created a 149 surface acre lake surrounded by National Forest lands. From Show Lo travel west on W. Duece of Clubs and turn right onto E. Linden Road. Travel for abou 2.5 miles and turn right. Take the first right (about .7 miles) and the destination wi be on the left.

Today, visitors can camp among the tall pines and hike along the lake at a coc 6,300 feet in elevation. Year-round camping, fishing, picnicking, boating, and wildlif viewing opportunities make Fool Hollow Lake Recreation Area a popular place.

Camping in fool hollow lake recreation area: Imagine camping among 100-foot pine trees beside a quiet lake watching majestic great blue herons at a cool 6,300 feet in elevation. There are 31 tent camping sites and 92 RV campground sites with water and electric hookups. Other amenities and conveniences include two boat ramps, two fish-cleaning stations, picnic tables, barrier-free restrooms, showers, drinking water, a dump station, four fishing piers, ten single-family picnic ramadas, and five large group ramadas that can handle 150 people. The west side boat ramp and parking is free for day users.

Hiking and Swimming: There is a 1.5-mile hiking trail along the lake. Access to the 103 miles of the White Mountain Trail System is available within 15 miles of the Recreation Area. Swimming is allowed from the shore or from boats, but there is no designated or patrolled swimming area.

Boating and Fishing: Both shoreline and boat fishing are available. Boat ramps are located on the east side and west side of the lake. Gasoline engines are limited to

10 HP. Fish species present include channel catfish, bluegill, black crappie rainbow trout, walleye, northern pike, and small and largemouth bass. All Arizona boating laws apply. Fishing is allowed for licensed fishermen (age 14 and up). There are 5 fish cleaning stations.

Wildlife Viewing: The area includes pine forest, wetland/riparian, and lacustrine habitat which provide viewing opportunities for numerous species. Waterfowl such as various ducks and geese, herons, egrets, and ibis are present seasonally. Neotropical birds such as bluebirds, goldfinches, and Stellar's jays are also present seasonally. Wintering bald eagles and summering ospreys and goshawks can be seen. Common mammals would include various squirrels, raccoons, beavers, and even elk and deer. Reptiles include various lizards and king snakes.

« Climb mountains not so the world can see you, but so you can see the world. »
- David McCullough Jr.

DATE(S) VISITED:

WEATHER:

☐ ☐ ☐ ☐ ☐

SEASON:

☐ ☐ ☐ ☐

COMPANIONS:

_____

_____

_____

_____

SPECIAL MEMORIES:

_____

_____

_____

_____

_____

_____

_____

_____

_____

SIGHTS:

_____

_____

_____

_____

_____

_____

_____

_____

NOTES: _____

_____

_____

_____

_____

_____

_____

_____

_____

_____

PHOTOS, STAMPS:

RATING: / 10   WILL RETURN?   YES / NO

CAMPING IN HAVASU FALLS
36.2552° N, 112.6979° W

Visiting Havasu Falls in the Grand Canyon is an unforgettable adventure that shou
be on your bucket list. it is a perfect place to explore and relax. The Havasup
Falls camping experience will be an adventure by itself. Marked by incredibly cle
turquoise water and brilliant red rock faces, Havasupai is the land that time forg
You can almost expect to see prehistoric creatures roaming through the trees. Pa
of the beauty of this land is that it's sheltered, remote, undeveloped, and untouche
by modern technology – and should stay that way! There are 5 amazing waterfalls
Havasupai.

BEST TIMES TO VISIT:
The best time visit to Havasu Falls is either in early spring or late autumn when th
temperature is perfect for hiking, and the conditions are pleasant enough for campin
In the summer it's even better camping weather, but you need to start your hike ear
in the morning due to the heat.

A QUICK GUIDE TO CAMPING IN HAVASU FALLS:
The trailhead for hiking to Havasu Falls begins at Hualapai Hilltop. To access th
area from Lake Havasu City, go north on Arizona 95, then east on Interstate 4
Access Route 66 either by (1) going north on East Andy Devine Ave./Route 66
Kingman, (2) or going north on Hackberry Rd./Hwy. 141, or (3) going north on Rou
66 in Seligman. Go north on Indian Road 18/Hualapai Hilltop Hwy and continu
for approximately 65 miles to the end of Indian Road 18, which drops you at th
Hualapai Hilltop parking area. It's about a 4 to 5-hour drive from Lake Havasu Cit
depending on your route and speed of travel. From Lake Havasu City to the trailhea
is approximately 175 miles via the Kingman/Route 66 route.

From the parking lot, the hike starts off steep and winds down switchbacks for at least 1½ miles. The trail is rugged and rocky so wear well-fitting and comfortable hiking boots or hiking shoes. The trail carves through a narrow canyon as you make your way to the village. Please listen and watch out for mule pack trains that frequent the trail during tourist season. Wearing headphones while hiking in is not recommended. you'll hear and see the creek water. Follow it downstream and make sure you cross the bridge to connect to the trail leading to the village.

What you'll need:
• A permit. A prior reservation to either the campground or the Lodge
• Good hiking shoes and a pair of water shoes or rubber sandals
• Bring sunscreen, a hat, a first-aid kit, snacks, and plenty of water. There is no water available on the trail

• For your stay at the bottom of the canyon, bring a bathing suit, water shoes, towel, and camera. Pack a tent, sleeping bag, sleeping pad, inflatable pillow, and portable backpacking stove if you are camping. Bring food even if you are staying at the Lodge.

Where to stay: The campground is an area spanning a mile on both sides of Havasu Creek between Havasu Falls and nearby Mooney Falls. There are no assigned sites; meaning, once you arrive, you're welcome to set up camp wherever you like within the designated area.

« You go away for a long time and return a different person you never come all the way back. »
- Paul Theroux

DATE(S) VISITED:

WEATHER:

☐ ☐ ☐ ☐ ☐

SEASON:

☐ ☐ ☐ ☐

COMPANIONS:

SPECIAL MEMORIES:

SIGHTS:

NOTES: _____

_____

_____

_____

_____

_____

_____

_____

_____

_____

_____

_____

PHOTOS, STAMPS:

RATING: ___ / 10   WILL RETURN?   YES / NO

FOSSIL CREEK WATERFALL
34.4147° N, 111.6055° W

This is one of the most accessible and beautiful places in all of Arizona. You ma
have never known that just two hours from Phoenix you can easily walk up to
stunning waterfall and see water that you would never think existed in this countr
While it is not Havasupai falls, it still offers a little glimpse of the stunning blue wate
meandering through the valley. While the "hike" is really short you can make it longe
by taking your time along the creek walk and climbing up past the waterfalls an
hiking up the stream beyond the falls. It truly is something you must see as there is
ton of fun at the falls. Whether you want to just lay in the water, rope swing, cliff jum
hike up past the falls, or even go into the grotto behind the waterfalls! It is truly a
oasis in the desert that you have to see.

BEST TIMES TO VISIT:
The best time to visit is Spring (March through May), the season feels moderate.

A QUICK GUIDE TO VISITING FOSSIL CREEK WATERFALL:
To access the Fossil Creek Waterfall Trailhead, you will take Interstate 17 whic
connects Phoenix to Flagstaff. From Phoenix, you will exit 287 off of interstate 17 an
turn towards State Route 260. From there, the road is paved for about 24 miles. On th
right side, you will come across Forest Road 708, which will have a Fossil Creek Sig
in front. Next is to travel 14 miles down a bumpy dirt road as you drop down 1,600 fee
in elevation. A 4 wheel drive vehicle is preferred, but you can do it with a normal ca
as long as it is not lowered and you drive the road slow around 5-10 mph. Getting t
the Fossil Springs Trailhead from Interstate 17, you will exit 287 towards Payson. Th
will take you on a 34-mile paved road to State Route 87. Go South on 87 for about
miles till you come to Fossil Creek Road (Forest Road 708). From there you follow th

road down to the Fossil Springs Trailhead where you will park and hike down to the springs.

Best Hikes & Trails: Fossil Creek is known far and wide as the trail to set foot on if you're looking for waterfalls and red rocks. There are a variety of trailheads that lead you to the creek, but this trail is the longest at a little over 8 miles.

Trail Stats: Length: 9 miles.
Trail Type: Out and back; Loose Rock and Boulders.
Elevation Gain/Loss: 1,486 feet.
Difficulty: Hard.
Kid-Friendly: No.
Dog-Friendly: Yes (must have a leash!).
Accessibility: 30 parking spaces at each trailhead! (There are 9 trailheads!).
Fee/Permit: Permit required during peak season (March 1 to October 1).

The hike down to the creek is fairly easy. Starting early in the day, you will find the sun on your backs and relatively shaded by the trees on either side as you descend down into the canyon. You'll arrive at an open section of the trail with large rocks

and pools that may or may not be filled with water depending on how hot the last few weeks have been. Continue on past the first sight of water and follow the trail down to a fork in the trail. You can either choose to go the creek route, which is quieter and less visited or visit the dam to the right. Once you get to your destination, creek or dam, prop up your Chacos and rejoice in the water you rarely see in Arizona. The hike back up will leave you winded. The heat of the summer sun will be beating down on you by midday, so be sure to pack enough sunscreen and water. Your water will go fast as you ascend, so overpacking water on the way down is a good idea. Hiking this trail is rewarding but also one that can be easily underestimated. Hanging out all day in the sun near the falls is fun, but it can drain you! Be safe and make sure you bring someone along to motivate you if you're not used to hiking in the Arizona heat.

« Travel has a way of stretching the mind. »
- Ralph Crawshaw

DATE(S) VISITED:

WEATHER:

☐   ☐   ☐   ☐   ☐

SEASON:

☐   ☐   ☐   ☐

COMPANIONS:

_____

_____

_____

SPECIAL MEMORIES:

_____

_____

_____

_____

_____

_____

_____

_____

SIGHTS:

_____

_____

_____

_____

_____

_____

_____

_____

NOTES: _____
_____
_____
_____
_____
_____
_____
_____
_____
_____
_____

PHOTOS, STAMPS:

RATING: / 10   WILL RETURN?   YES / NO

TANQUE VERDE FALLS
32.254982° N, 110.655338° W

East of Tucson, a creek tumbles through a steep canyon of the Rincon Mountain Water falling from the high country down to the desert means one thing: waterfall This is Tanque Verde Creek, and the waterfalls it has. The name Tanque Verde Fal refers to the highest and most impressive one, an 80-footer that drops into a larg pool, but you'll pass many smaller cascades on the hike to reach it. This spot make a magical swimming hole on a hot day when the falls are flowing. Though the po holds water year-round, the creek and waterfall run only seasonally.

BEST TIMES TO VISIT:
The best time to visit is from March to October. But spring and early summer off more opportunities to see the falls flowing.

A QUICK GUIDE TO VISITING TANQUE VERDE FALLS:
Don't let the distance or elevation profile of the hike fool you; it's not as easy as seems. That's because most of the way is not walking on a trail, but boulder hoppin and scrambling up the creekbed. It begins on a trail that switchbacks down into th canyon. Be sure to follow the switchbacks, do not cut straight downhill as some peopl have clearly done, because this causes undue erosion to the slope. Soon enough you be in the wash at the bottom. If water is flowing there, the falls will certainly be runnin

Even there at the end of the trail makes a great place to dip your feet and relax. short distance upstream is a gravel beach and fine wading pool. Continuing farthe requires more strenuous hiking. Most of the way is on loose gravel and slipper granite, with places that require using your hands. If you're confident in you scrambling abilities, keep ongoing. There is no defined trail, so you must navigate th path of least resistance around obstacles and crossings of the creek. You'll encounter several pretty waterfalls and swimming holes as you ascend the wash, but the main falls take a little more work. The final major obstacle comes at a 30-foot waterfall in a slot behind a wedged boulder. There you must climb a short, vertical section of rock or find a path up and around. Once above this waterfall, you'll see the main waterfall just ahead.

Tanque Verde Falls is a much different spectacle than anything previously on the hike. It's a tall, partially free-falling waterfall that shoots through a notch. The cliffs on either side make an amphitheater filled with red-tinged water at the bottom. The color comes from tannins in the roots of mesquite and other plants which grow throughout miles of the wash upstream. Though the color looks a bit unnatural, there is nothing wrong with it. Though the cliffs may be tempting for jumping, use extreme caution. The pool is not deep everywhere, and currents beneath the falls can be strong.

If you want to swim close to the falls or climb on the cliffs, do so at your own risk and be aware of others around you. To play it safe, stay at the pool's end where the water is shallow and the bank gently sloped. There is room on flat rocks and a small gravel beach for lots of people to spread out and relax. This place is quite popular on nice

 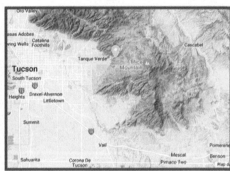

days over the weekend. On weekdays or less-than-ideal weather days, however, you may find it all to yourself.

Best Trails: Length: 3.1 km. - Elevation gain: 141 m - **Route type:** Out & back.
Explore this 1.90 mile, out and back trail near Tucson, Arizona. Generally considered a moderately challenging route, it takes an average of 1 h 5 min to complete. This is a very popular area for hiking, so you'll likely encounter other people while exploring. The trail is open year-round and is beautiful to visit anytime. Dogs are welcome but must be on a leash.

What should I wear: comfortable, closed-toe shoes or boots - waterproof preferred - a wide-brimmed hat or visor - light layers - sunscreen - sunglasses.

« *It's a big world out there. It would be a shame not to experience it.* »
- J. D. Andrews

DATE(S) VISITED:

WEATHER:

☐ ☐ ☐ ☐ ☐

SEASON:

☐ ☐ ☐ ☐

COMPANIONS:

SPECIAL MEMORIES:

SIGHTS:

NOTES: _____

_____

_____

_____

_____

_____

_____

_____

_____

_____

PHOTOS, STAMPS:

RATING: / 10   WILL RETURN?   YES / NO

CAMELBACK MOUNTAIN
33.5151° N, 111.9619° W

Located next to, and partially within, Big Pocono State Park. Camelback Mountai
Resort is a popular ski and snowboard resort located in the Pocono Mountains near th
town of Tannersville, Monroe County, Pennsylvania. Camelback Mountain's highe
peak Big Pocono reaches an elevation of 2,133 feet. The resort has 166 acres of skiin
and snowboarding terrain. There are 35 slopes on the mountain, with the longest, th
Nile Mile, one mile long and with a vertical drop of 800 feet. There are 15 lifts and tw
high-speed detachable chairlifts. Camelback is Poconos Mountain's largest ski reso
There are also two terrain parks and the only Half Pipe in the Poconos. The reso
also has an indoor and outdoor water park, named Camelbeach. The indoor park
open year-round. Camelbeach includes 37 waterslides, four body slides, a mat slid
five-tube slides, and four raft rides. There is also a 30,000-square-foot wave pool, laz
river, a children's play area, and a full-sized competition pool.

BEST TIMES TO VISIT:
The best times to climb Camelback are the late fall, winter, and early sprin
November's average highs are in the mid-70s, while December and January's high
are in the 60s.

A QUICK GUIDE TO VISITING CAMELBACK MOUNTAIN:
Best Hikes & Trails:
Hiking Cholla Trail Camelback Mountain: Cholla Trail is an excellent choice fc
a moderate to somewhat difficult hike on the Camelback Mountain hiking trails!
takes about a 1.5 hours round-trip for hikers in good physical condition. Feast you
eyes on breathtaking panoramic views of Scottsdale and Paradise Valley as you follo
the trail along the spine of the camel's back, winding west toward the top of the hum

(and the highest point of elevation on Camelback Mountain).

Slowly, you'll reach what feels like the culmination of your Camelback Mountain hike – you're about halfway, There at the saddle, opt for a moment of serenity at the sudden exposure to downtown Phoenix in the desert's distance. If you're pressed on time or feeling out of shape, this is a great ascension point to reach and from which to retreat. The next part of the climb gets difficult and following the trail marks isn't as easy-start hiking the camel's hump and there can be some steep moments! Many times, you need to use your hands to climb. Hydrate, pay attention to your surroundings, and keep an eagle's eye out for trail marks. The final ascent will bring you up the east side of the Camel's hump. Take a big boost of self-confidence: you're strong to have made it this far and so close to the top.

Hiking Echo Canyon Trail: The Echo trail gets right to the workout, right away. The dusty path may look like it winds gently up toward the camel's head, but pace yourself, obstacles are to come! Reach your first viewpoint at the end of the dirt trail, facing northwest and down at Paradise Valley. To your right, your first challenge awaits you: the Steps. The Steps bring you behind the camel's head to the handrails: a couple of short, steep, rocky paths. Both are assisted by handrails- use them. The steps bring you to the south side of the camel's neck- the third, non-official handrail- another short, rocky portion with no actual handrails. Enjoy your first Phoenix-facing view

there and gear up as you follow the trail to the most strenuous portion of your climb: Take your time and take breaks as needed. Follow the rocks up to another segment of- you guessed it- the Rocks. Make it up this last segment and you're 9/10s of the way to the top. Enjoy another beautiful view of Phoenix and remind yourself that in less than about ten minutes to the top, you'll have summited Echo Canyon.

* Note: Trailhead hours are sunrise to sunset, so plan your hike accordingly. Also, if you're traveling with a family pet, remember that dogs are prohibited at all Echo Canyon and Cholla trail areas. N64Camelback Mountain is closed from 11 a.m. to 5 p.m. on days with excessive heat warnings. There are no public restrooms or drinking fountains at the trailhead.

« Fill your life with experiences, not things. Have stories to tell, not stuff to show. »
- Unknown

DATE(S) VISITED:

WEATHER:

☐ ☐ ☐ ☐ ☐

SEASON:

☐ ☐ ☐ ☐

COMPANIONS:

SPECIAL MEMORIES:

SIGHTS:

NOTES: _____

_____

_____

_____

_____

_____

_____

_____

_____

_____

PHOTOS, STAMPS:

RATING: / 10   WILL RETURN?   YES / NO

MOUNT LEMMON
32.4432° N, 110.7577° W

Regarded as one of the most scenic drives in southeast Arizona, the Mount Lemmo Scenic Byway takes travelers to the upper reaches of Mount Lemmon and th Santa Catalina Range. Aside from the arresting canyon and mountain views, th nearly 60-mile round-trip byway offers visitors the biological equivalent of drivin from the deserts of Mexico to the forests of Canada (the road begins in the lowe Sonoran vegetative life zone and ascends to the high forests in the Canadian zone Approximately an hour's drive from Tucson's city center, Mount Lemmon is a favori day trip and camping spot for Tucsonans. It's a beautiful outdoor escape - ideal fc hiking, biking, rock-climbing, picnicking, sunset-watching, and sledding/skiing. Fu for the whole family. Mt. Lemmon is usually 20-30 degrees cooler than Tucson, so yc can find cooler temperatures there in the summer and a beautiful layer of snow in th winter, along with vibrantly colored leaves in autumn.

BEST TIMES TO VISIT:

Mt. Lemmon is always a good idea! In the spring and summer, you can escape th heat in a tent or cabin or at a picnic. You can bask in the gorgeous fall colors in th autumn and you can enjoy the snow in the winter.

A QUICK GUIDE TO VISITING MOUNT LEMMON:

Mt. Lemmon is a peak in the Catalina mountain range, surrounded by Coronad National Forest. To reach Mt. Lemmon from Tucson, turn off Tanque Verde Roa onto Catalina Highway. Take Catalina Highway as far up the mountain as you desi to go. On your way up the mountain, you may want to stop at Windy Point Vista (Mi Marker 14). This popular lookout point has bathrooms and is a terrific spot for photo

Best Hikes & Trails:

Aspen and Marshall Gulch trails: This loop hike is ideal for an active afternoon stroll. The route, which covers about 3.7 miles, takes you through a meadow of wildflowers and gives you mountain views. For a shorter hike, take the 2.6-mile out-and-back Marshall Gulch Trail.

Bug Springs Trail: The secret to being successful on this steep hike is simple: Go early. The 9.5-mile out-and-back trail — heavily trafficked by mountain bikers and hikers alike — starts on the lower end of the mountain, so it's essential to start before the heat hits. Taking hikers through a variety of terrain, the trail dips in and out of the pines and also features hoodoos — massive rock formations — scattered along the mountain. The trailhead is 12.2 miles up Catalina Highway. Look for the signs marking the start of the trail.

Butterfly Trail: If you're looking for an all-day hike, this 11.5-mile round-trip trek is for you. Rated moderate by AllTrails, the Butterfly Trail takes you through the alpine forest to Mount Bigelow, offering spectacular views of the backside of Mount Lemmon. If you look close enough, you might see some wreckage from an F-86 SABERjet that crashed in 1957. Veer onto an unofficial trail that breaks off at 2.6 miles in to find the site. The trailhead is 19 miles up Catalina Highway on the right side of the road.

Aspen Draw Trail: Starting at Mount Lemmon Ski Valley, this 1.7-mile winding trail climbs 843 feet to the top of the mountain. The hike takes you into a scene from an old fairy tale, as big old pine trees snake up the mountain. The best part? This hike is fully shaded. Once at the top, you can either head back down the trail or walk along the road back to return. The trail starts at the base of Mount Lemmon Ski Valley, about 19 miles up Catalina Highway.

Camping on Mount Lemmon: There are 5 general use campgrounds on Mt. Lemmon, plus 2 group sites. Public bathrooms are available in Summerhaven, at the major campgrounds, and at most trailheads.

« With age, comes wisdom. With travel, comes understanding. »
- Sandra Lake

DATE(S) VISITED:

WEATHER:

☐ ☐ ☐ ☐ ☐

SEASON:

☐ ☐ ☐ ☐

COMPANIONS: _____

_____

_____

_____

SPECIAL MEMORIES: _____

_____

_____

_____

_____

_____

_____

_____

_____

_____

SIGHTS: _____

_____

_____

_____

_____

_____

_____

_____

_____

_____
_____
_____
_____
_____
_____
_____
_____
_____
_____
_____

HOTOS, STAMPS:

RATING: / 10   WILL RETURN?   YES / NO

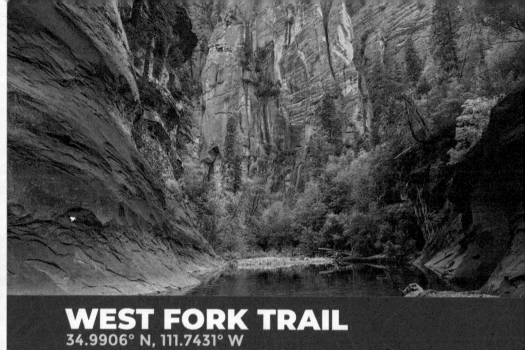

WEST FORK TRAIL
34.9906° N, 111.7431° W

There are a number of reasons why West Fork is the most popular trail on th
Coconino National Forest. You'll know some of them once you've strolled beside th
pleasant little stream that ripples along the canyon floor and looked up, way up, at th
dizzying cliffs that tower above it.

Length: 6.9 mi.
Elevation Gain/Loss: 839 ft.
Difficulty: Easy.

BEST TIMES TO VISIT:
Late spring and early Fall are excellent for avoiding crowds and for local site seein
June is a particularly pleasant and dry month, with high temperatures in the 70s⁵
(22°C) and very low rainfall.

A QUICK GUIDE TO VISITING WEST FORK TRAIL:
West fork trail is about 25 minutes from central Sedona. Once you're on State Rout
89A you'll stay on there for about 11 miles. You'll drive past the little Dairy Quee
and Slide Rock. The drive itself is stunning. There's not too much of a heads up fc
the turn into the parking lot, but it will be on your left if you're coming from Sedon
There is an entrance fee you have to pay to get into the parking lot.

Before you really get started on this hike you first cross over a small bridge and pas
by some historic ruins of what used to be Mayhew's Oak Creek Lodge. These ar
both great spots to take pictures at. This should only take you about 2-3 hours t
hike, but you'll most likely want to spend all day there. On this trail, you will be hikin

alongside and crossing over the creek. There are many spots where you have to cross the creek but there are strategically placed rocks in the water for you to hop across. The rocks are very slippery and usually wobbly, so don't be surprised if you lose your footing and end up ankles deep in the creek. It's all a good time though. This is about a 7-mile hike, it has a steady incline you don't really notice and the hike goes by rather quickly. This is by far the most uniquely beautiful hike Sedona has to offer. Every part of this hike is stunning. From the red rocks that are reaching up to the sky to the greenery decorating the Creekside. This is a great hike for children because the creek usually didn't get deeper than ankle-high. This is also a great hike to take your dogs on since it's mainly shaded and has the water for them to cool off in.

* Hiking Tips: Bring shoes you don't mind getting wet and a change of socks for the car ride back. Water and snacks are a must.

Once you get to the end of the maintained trail you can actually venture on further. If you've managed to keep your feet dry up until this point, this surely will change if you choose to go on! I highly recommend going further, even if it's only a couple hundred feet. The canyon walls start to close around you and this makes for an insane picture. Once you start heading back you'll take in all the views you missed. You realize you've

become a pro at jumping from rock to rock since you end up doing it over a dozen times each way. This is one of those hikes where you get a little sad when you see the parking lot because you have to go home now. West fork trail is about 25 minutes from central Sedona. Once you're on State Route 89A you'll stay on there for about 11 miles. You'll drive past the little Dairy Queen and Slide Rock. The drive itself is stunning. There's not too much of a heads up for the turn into the parking lot, but it will be on your left if you're coming from Sedona.

« We wander for distraction, but we travel for fulfillment. »
- Hilaire Belloc

DATE(S) VISITED:

WEATHER:

☐ ☐ ☐ ☐ ☐

SEASON:

☐ ☐ ☐ ☐

COMPANIONS:

_____

_____

_____

_____

SPECIAL MEMORIES:

_____

_____

_____

_____

_____

_____

_____

_____

_____

SIGHTS:

_____

_____

_____

_____

_____

_____

_____

_____

_____

NOTES: _____
_____
_____
_____
_____
_____
_____
_____
_____
_____
_____

PHOTOS, STAMPS:

RATING: / 10   WILL RETURN?   YES / NO

OTHER POINTS
OF INTEREST

Arizona is a year-round destination that piques the imagination and inspires the soul with its dramatic landscape.

The state is nothing less than stunning, with a lot of to see and experience. In this part, we have for you the best Arizona mix, these places were chosen from hundreds literally. So you can't miss it when you're in the state.

PLAN IT | DO IT | JOURNAL IT

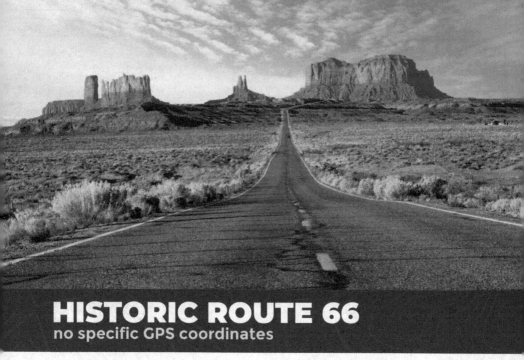

HISTORIC ROUTE 66
no specific GPS coordinates

"America's Highway," "The Road to Opportunity," "Mother Road" — All nicknames for Route 66, the most famous highway in American history and the first-ever artery connecting the east coast to the west coast. Route 66 is an iconic highway with many fun stops and sights to see along the way. The Arizona segments offer diverse scenery and milder temperatures compared to the driving monotony and seasonal heat in the California desert. Route 66 skirts the Grand Canyon east of Kingman, offering access to touring opportunities in the Hualapai and Havasupai nations. Kingman, the southern gateway to Hoover Dam and Las Vegas, is often considered the heart of Historic Route 66 with its numerous attractions and convenient location. Also, the Historic Route 66 Association of Arizona actively promotes the route. Northwest Arizona features two long segments of Historic Route 66 that veer well away from Interstate-40. Going west to east, the first is a 53-mile stretch from the Topock exit (mile 1) on I-40 to Kingman, Arizona. It features beautiful desert mountain scenery and an old west town that refused to die. The second is a roughly 110-mile segment from Kingman to just west of Ash Fork, Arizona.

BEST TIMES TO VISIT:
The best time to take a Route 66 road trip is between April (late spring) to early July (early summer), and then, after the summer break/summer holidays.

A QUICK GUIDE TO VISITING HISTORIC ROUTE 66:
North of Golden Shores, the route soon starts heading into the mountains with very scenic driving before reaching the historic old west town of Oatman, snuggled in the mountains. The town largely features its original buildings, including its main attraction, the Oatman Hotel. Take a day trip to The Nature Park with 175 acres, home

150 animals, including monkeys, tigers, bears, livestock, reptiles, a variety of birds, and a rare Siberian Tiger.

Stops Along Route 66:

Diamond Creek Road to the Colorado River: Located off Route 66 in Peach Springs, Diamond Creek Road is an adventurous "road less traveled" to the Colorado River. You will actually be driving down into the Grand Canyon to the Colorado River. Bring a picnic lunch and enjoy nature at its grandest.

Grand Canyon Caverns: A must-see day trip, this natural wonder was created over a period of 35 million years and is the largest dry cavern in the U.S. The air in the caverns is a consistent 56° year-round due to zero humidity and is drawn in from the Grand Canyon through 60 miles of limestone caves and crevasses.

Havasu Falls: A beautiful tropical paradise awaits you. Mistakenly thought to be a part of Lake Havasu, Havasu Falls is a part of the Grand Canyon and about 176 miles from the London Bridge. Havasu Falls is a major destination for hikers and those looking for a challenging, yet rewarding outdoor vacation.

Keepers of the Wild: is dedicated to the dignified rescue of exotic animals. Take a day trip to The Nature Park with 175 acres, home to 150 animals, including monkeys, tigers, bears, livestock, reptiles, a variety of birds, and a rare Siberian Tiger.

Route 66 Museum/Powerhouse Visitor Center, Kingman: The Route 66 Museum is truly unique in that it is a museum of history, located in the "heart" of the longest remaining stretch of the 2400 miles that was Route 66. The brilliant murals, photos, and life-size dioramas capture each of the groups that have traveled the route that's known as the Mother Road.

Route 66 Facts: Arizona contains the longest unbroken stretch of Route 66 still in existence, 158 miles from west of Ash Fork to the California border.
The only National Park that Route 66 passes through is Petrified Forest National Park in Arizona.
The longest curve, the steepest grade, and the highest point on Route 66 are in Arizona.

« Two roads diverged in a wood and I – I took the one less traveled by. »
- Robert Frost

DATE(S) VISITED:

WEATHER:

☐ ☐ ☐ ☐ ☐

SEASON:

☐ ☐ ☐ ☐

COMPANIONS: _____

_____

_____

SPECIAL MEMORIES: _____

_____

_____

_____

_____

_____

_____

_____

SIGHTS: _____

_____

_____

_____

_____

_____

_____

_____

_____

NOTES: _____

_____

_____

_____

_____

_____

_____

_____

_____

_____

PHOTOS, STAMPS:

RATING: / 10	WILL RETURN? YES / NO

HOOVER DAM
36.0137° N, 114.7317° W

The Hoover Dam is one of the greatest feats of engineering in the United States, and it is still among the most iconic structures of the Southwest today. The Hoover Dam was constructed in the 1930s. It is a National Historic Landmark and is considered to be one of the Seven Modern Civil Engineering Wonders. A surefire way to enjoy your visit to the Hoover Dam is to check out one or more of the lookout platforms. The Hoover Dam Lookout on the Arizona side of the dam offers aerial views of Hoover Dam that will leave you breathless. Without a doubt, it's the best way to comprehend the immense size of this structure. You'll simultaneously get a look at the rushing water, Lake Mead, Black Canyon, and the surrounding desert environment.

BEST TIMES TO VISIT:
The best time to visit is between March and April during the spring and fall seasons. And the least busy time of day for tours is from 9 a.m. until 10:30 a.m., as well as 3:00 p.m. until 3:45 p.m. To enjoy the site entirely, we recommend visitors arrive by 2:00 p.m. The dam closes at 9 p.m. Traffic around the dam during holidays and weekends can be extremely heavy with long delays on the roadway.

A QUICK GUIDE TO VISITING HOOVER DAM:
Hoover Dam straddles the Nevada-Arizona state line. The road over the dam used to be part of the main highway through that area, but now it ends on the Arizona side. It is easy to spend an hour or more just walking on and around the dam itself. The state line marker is a popular photo op and it's fun to get a good look at Lake Mead on one side and then wonder at a HUGE drop down the concrete wall on the other. There is a statuary on the Nevada side where you can get an idea of just how challenging Hoover Dam was to build and how many lives were lost for it. There is a gift shop and

ife. It costs nothing to visit Hoover Dam. There is a charge to take a tour and see e visitor center. Admission to the visitor center is included with a tour or can be urchased separately.

on't Miss the Bridge: About a mile before you reach Hoover Dam, look for a arking lot near the Mike O'Callaghan-Pat Tillman Memorial Bridge. This bridge, hich was completed in 2010, spans the gorge in front of Hoover Dam. The bridge is 1 engineering feat on its own and there is an informative footpath up to the bridge nd a pedestrian walkway across it. You can get great photos of the bridge from oover Dam and of Hoover Dam from the bridge. There is only one small parking t at the bridge, compared with hundreds of spaces at the dam. To beat the crowds, onsider stopping at the bridge first if you arrive in the morning, or last if you arrive the afternoon.

oover Dam History & Fact: The dam was built between 1931 and 1936. Its original urpose was to hold back the waters of the Colorado River and supply hydroelectric ower to the surrounding area, which was rapidly developing. Today, the dam still lfills this purpose and provides power to over a million people in three states, and rigates 2 million acres of land.

The Hoover Dam's height of 726.4 ft made it the world's tallest dam until 1968 when was surpassed by California's Orville Dam (770 ft).
The Mike O'Callaghan – Pat Tillman Memorial Bridge is the Western Hemisphere's ngest single-span concrete arch bridge. It replaced the portion of US-93 that crossed ver the top of the dam since it often got too congested.
The construction of the Hoover Dam was a huge project and provided employment or thousands of people who were out of work due to the Great Depression. As these borers flocked to the area, they needed a place to live, so Boulder City was built to ouse the workforce.
The dam is named after U.S. President Herbert Hoover, whose administration pproved the project's construction. However, President Hoover wasn't invited to the edication ceremony, and the dam wasn't officially named until 1947.

« *There are no foreign lands. It is the traveler only who is foreign.* »
- Robert Louis Stevenson

DATE(S) VISITED:

WEATHER:

☐ ☐ ☐ ☐ ☐

SEASON:

☐ ☐ ☐ ☐

COMPANIONS: _____

_____

_____

_____

SPECIAL MEMORIES: _____

_____

_____

_____

_____

_____

_____

_____

_____

SIGHTS: _____

_____

_____

_____

_____

_____

_____

_____

_____

PHOTOS, STAMPS:

RATING: / 10   WILL RETURN?   YES / NO

METEOR CRATER
35.0278° N, 111.0222° W

Visit the world's best-preserved meteorite impact site on Earth. Located just minutes from Interstate 40 and the old Route 66 in Northern Arizona near Winslow. Meteor Crater is the spectacular result of a collision that rocked the American Southwest approximately 50,000 years ago with the energy of more than 20 million tons of TNT. Situated under the wide skies of the Arizona High Desert, Meteor Crater offers an interactive educational experience for the entire family in a beautiful, natural setting. Be sure to stop at the Meteor Crater Visitor Center located on the rim of the Crater. The fully air-conditioned building features an 80-seat widescreen theater, indoor crater viewing area, Crater Trail access, Interactive Discovery Center, artifacts and exhibits, gift and mineral Shop, "Collision!" 4D Experience Room, and the Blasted Bistro.

BEST TIMES TO VISIT:
The temperatures in Meteor Crater Natural Landmark are typically more comfortable during April, May, September, and October months. Our suggestion would be to visit us in the late morning (anytime after 10 am) or in the afternoon.

A QUICK GUIDE TO VISITING METEOR CRATER NATURAL LANDMARK:
If you follow the signs in the visitor center to the rim, you can step outside and look upon this preserved crater from decks that overlook it. There are several platforms to gaze down upon the impact site, some allowing a little different view. You can only stand on the ground next to the crater if you sign up for a guided tour at the visitor center. the most interesting views of Meteor Crater are those through the permanent telescopes. On one platform overlooking the crater, there are telescopes pointed in certain directions, with names next to the telescopes, stating what you should look for.

hen you look through the telescopes, you get a better sense of how far away certain ndmarks are within the crater. Some old mining equipment still sits in the middle the depression; seeing it so small in the telescope gives one a better reference to w far away you actually are. The crater is big, but it's hard to judge just how big it is hen standing at the rim.

ke most of this area, Spring and Fall have the most pleasant weather, but there are door viewing areas for those hot summer days or cool winter temperatures. Meteor rater is a desert environment with low levels of precipitation and is characterized hot summers, mild winters with little snowfall, and very pleasant spring and fall asons.

teresting Facts about Meteor Crater:

Its name, the "Meteor Crater" originally comes from the nearby post office with e name "Meteor, Arizona." The US Board on Geographic Names gives names to atural features based on the name of the nearest post office. Other names the crater known by including Canyon Diablo Crater and Barringer Crater.
The Meteor Crater was designated a Natural Landmark in 1967, as the world's first entified meteor crater.

The square-like appearance of the crater is believed to be caused by cracks that ready existed in the earth's layers.
During the 1960s and 70s, NASA astronauts performed training maneuvers in the rater for the Apollo moon missions.
There is an RV park on the property with room for 71 RVs.
There are also dog kennels available at the visitor center if you are traveling with our dog.

« People don't take trips — trips take people. »
- John Steinbeck

DATE(S) VISITED:

WEATHER:

☐ ☐ ☐ ☐ ☐

SEASON:

☐ ☐ ☐ ☐

COMPANIONS:

_____
_____
_____
_____

SPECIAL MEMORIES:

_____
_____
_____
_____
_____
_____
_____
_____
_____

SIGHTS:

_____
_____
_____
_____
_____
_____
_____
_____
_____

NOTES: _____
_____
_____
_____
_____
_____
_____
_____
_____
_____
_____

PHOTOS, STAMPS:

RATING: / 10   **WILL RETURN?**   YES / NO

DESERT BOTANICAL GARDEN
33.4618° N, 111.9446° W

Located in Papago Park, not far from downtown Phoenix, the Desert Botanical Garden is a Phoenix Point of Pride and one of only 24 botanical gardens accredited by the American Alliance of Museums. Unlike most botanical gardens, it focuses on the plants that thrive in—and to a lesser extent, the animals and people that live in—the Sonoran Desert, which surrounds the city. this botanic garden is a beautiful and restful place, displaying more than 20,000 desert plants from around the world. The walk called Plants and People of the Sonoran Desert Trail is the state's best introduction to southwestern ethnobotany (human use of plants). Along this trail, you can make your own yucca-fiber brush and practice grinding corn as Native Americans once did. On the Desert Wildflower Trail, you'll find colorful wildflowers throughout much of the year. Each spring, there's usually a butterfly pavilion filled with live butterflies. If you come late in the day, you can stay until after dark and see night-blooming flowers and dramatically lit cacti. A cafe on the grounds makes a great lunch spot.

BEST TIMES TO VISIT:
The best time to visit is November through April. The garden is typically open from 8 a.m. to 8 p.m. daily. To beat the crowds, arrive right when the garden opens or later in the afternoon.

A QUICK GUIDE TO VISITING DESERT BOTANICAL GARDEN:
The Desert Botanical Garden is located at 1201 N. Galvin Parkway. By car, take the 202 to Priest Drive, which becomes Galvin Parkway. Head north through the Van Buren Street intersection before driving through the first roundabout. At the second roundabout, turn right and continue to the parking lot. Alternatively, you can take Loop 101 to McDowell Road and turn west. Continue six blocks to Galvin Parkway,

ke a left, and then another left at the first roundabout. Parking is free. If you're using
ublic transportation, take the light rail to the Washington/Priest Station and transfer
Bus 56 north. The bus stops in the garden's parking lot.

isit the Butterfly Pavilion: Usually open for several weeks in the fall and spring,
e Butterfly Pavilion contains hundreds of butterflies, including Monarchs, that
ve in the Southwest. Visitors can learn about the pollinators and pose for pictures
the pavilion as butterflies flutter around them. An activity book for kids can be
ownloaded before your visit. Admission to the Butterfly Pavilion is free with general
dmission, although you will need to reserve a time to visit.

ine at Gertrude's: This award-winning restaurant serves up New American fare
very day of the week. With a seasonal menu focusing on locally-sourced ingredients,
xpect entrées like green chili cheeseburgers, duck enchiladas, and lamb curry.

xplore the Garden's Indoor Offerings: When you're in need of some shade, check
ut the 9,000-book library dedicated to native desert plants, as well as the gift shop
r gardening and desert-related souvenirs.

heck Out an Event: Special events draw people to the garden year-round.
est Hikes & Trails:
esert Discovery Loop Trail: Start your visit on the Desert Discovery Loop Trail, just

f the Ottosen Entry Garden. Palo verde trees, along with a mix of cacti and succulents
om around the world, line the loop. Don't miss the Kitchell Family Heritage Garden,
hich showcases the plants found in Baja California. From the Desert Discovery Loop
rail, you can branch-off to all but the Desert Wildflower Loop Trail.
lants & People of the Sonoran Desert Loop Trail: You'll learn how plants have been
sed for food, medicine, and building materials, in addition to seeing examples of
ohono O'odham, Western Apache, and Hispanic households.
esert Wildflower Loop Trail: During the spring, yellow, orange, pink, and purple
lossoms color the 0.3-mile loop. Take this loop to visit the Butterfly Pavilion.
onoran Desert Nature Loop Trail: This trail offers incredible views of Phoenix and
e surrounding mountains.
enter for Desert Living Trail: This trail explores sustainability.

« Stop worrying about the potholes in the road and enjoy the journey. »
- Babs Hoffman

DATE(S) VISITED:

WEATHER:

☐ ☐ ☐ ☐ ☐

SEASON:

☐ ☐ ☐ ☐

COMPANIONS: _____

_____

_____

_____

SPECIAL MEMORIES: _____

_____

_____

_____

_____

_____

_____

_____

_____

_____

SIGHTS: _____

_____

_____

_____

_____

_____

_____

_____

_____

_____

NOTES:

_____
_____
_____
_____
_____
_____
_____
_____
_____
_____

PHOTOS, STAMPS:

RATING: / 10   WILL RETURN?   YES / NO

LAVA RIVER CAVE
35.3424° N, 111.8363° W

Visiting the Lava River Cave in Central Oregon near Bend is an adventure you must be prepared for if you want to truly enjoy it and marvel at the natural beauty. Interestingly, the lava tube was first recorded in 1889 by Leander Dillman. However, the presence of crafted obsidian flakes hints at earlier use by native Americans. It was presumably used for storing meat in the summer and perhaps even for winter shelter. Lava River Cave in Flagstaffwas formed by molten rock that erupted from a volcanic vent near Hart Prairie. As the lava flowed from the vent, the outside hardened into a tube-like formation. This newly created tunnel filled with molten lava created a fiery faucet. Once the flow was done, the cave cooled and remains a 3/4 mile-long tunnel for all of those brave enough to explore it.

BEST TIMES TO VISIT:

You can visit Lava River Cave year-round, though you may need to ski to it in winter since Forest Roads 245 and/or 171 are closed during the winter months. Temperatures inside the cave remain roughly the same in summer and winter (between 35° and 45° Fahrenheit). If you see information saying it is closed, check directly with Flagstaff Ranger District for current status information - 928-526-0866.

A QUICK GUIDE TO VISITING LAVA RIVER CAVE:

What to Bring: 3 sources of light. Yes, you really do want at least 2-3 light sources including a flashlight, headlamp, lantern, etc. This is because the rock floors are a painful combination of slippery and dark. If you fall or drop a light source catching yourself you are stuck in the pitch black of the lava tubes. This is no ordinary dark where you can slightly make out the rocks or have your eyes get used to the lack of light. It is dark where you cannot see your hand if it is touching your nose!

Bring steady shoes. This includes hiking boots, running shoes, etc.
Bring warm clothing. The cave is not only a constant average of 42°, but it leaks snowmelt and weather from rainstorms. This means the cold can be slightly damp depending on the time of year.
Optional-You could bring a helmet. This cave changes height frequently and in the dark, it is difficult to make out anything around your flashlight. Even the shortest of people have the potential to bang their heads on the wall if they are focused on the ground.

Drive 9 miles north of Flagstaff on US 180 and turn west (left) on FR 245 (at milepost 30). Continue 3 miles to FR171 and turn south 1 mile to where FR 171B turns left a short distance to Lava River Cave.

The road to the main parking lot is incredibly well-maintained. Any vehicle will have an easy time accessing the area. The approach from the parking lot to the entry of the Lava River cave is a flat, well-maintained, hard-packed trail that is less than 1/4 mile long. Being in a mostly good physical condition is appropriate. The first 300 ft of the cave is composed of loose, often times slippery boulder rocks that require some amount of scrambling. Using your hands, feet and even sitting on rocks for stability

at times is likely. The Lava River Cave meets all "Confined Space Entry" criteria, so be prepared for this at the beginning of your exploration. Once you are in the cave after scrambling down into it, the angle of the ground flattens out but the terrain will continue to be uneven for the remaining distance. There will be points in the cave where the roof gets low. Shorter humans can crouch as they walk, taller humans (maybe 6'2+) might need to crawl.
There is camping around the area but please remember to have your campsite at least 1 mile away from the cave entrance. The camping etiquette around the area includes picking up all trash, not feeding the wildlife (there are cows, deer, and elk that wander the area), and most importantly not defacing the cave walls. There have been many cases of graffiti in the cave and although they have been removed since it is obviously respectful to leave the area how it was when you first set foot on it.

« Though we travel the world over to find the beautiful,
we must carry it with us or we find it not. »
- Ralph Waldo Emerson

DATE(S) VISITED:

WEATHER:

☐ ☐ ☐ ☐ ☐

SEASON:

☐ ☐ ☐ ☐

COMPANIONS:

SPECIAL MEMORIES:

SIGHTS:

NOTES:

_____
_____
_____
_____
_____
_____
_____
_____
_____
_____

PHOTOS, STAMPS:

RATING: / 10   **WILL RETURN?**   YES / NO

LONDON BRIDGE
34.4716° N, 114.3475° W

Lake Havasu City is a sprawling desert oasis in Arizona, just two and a half hours southwest of Las Vegas, and within a half a day's drive of Joshua Tree, Death Valley, Saguaro, and Grand Canyon National Parks. There are so many things to do around Lake Havasu, but one of the coolest is to visit the historic London Bridge in Lake Havasu City, which has been open for car and pedestrian traffic since 1971. London Bridge has become a favorite among Arizona attractions. This 280 meters long bridge is ideally located near downtown the city and other exciting local attractions. While visiting this magnificent structure, visitors can witness the scars from World War II that mark the bridge's surface and enjoy the view over Lake Havasu with all the kinds of boats anchored in the shadow of this icon.

BEST TIMES TO VISIT:

Unless you really love the heat of the desert, it's best to avoid visiting Lake Havasu City in the summer, between June and September, when the temperatures top 100 degrees almost every day. Winter is great for outdoor activities like hiking and mountain biking, but the Lake will be too cold for all but the bravest swimmers. the best time to visit London Bridge is In April, the Spring.

A QUICK GUIDE TO VISITING LONDON BRIDGE, ARIZONA:

Lake Havasu was created long before the city — back in the 1930s when the Parker Dam was built on the Colorado River. Thirty years later, in 1963, chainsaw tycoon and millionaire, Robert McCulloch is rumored to have flown over the lake searching for a suitable location to test out his line of outboard motors. He went on to buy 3,500 acres of the desolate desert for under $75 an acre, and even though there were no major highways connecting Lake Havasu to the rest of the country, a beautiful city began to nerge out of the desert.

ondon Bridge is truly the heart of Lake Havasu City and many of the main attractions
e located within close proximity to the bridge. Even without a car, this part of Lake
avasu City features great beaches, bike trails, boat rentals, and more...

isit the Bridgewater Channel: The Channel is a narrow man-made waterway that
erves as a no-wake spot for the parade of boats that slowly travel through. There are
andy beaches and parks on either side of the channel, not to mention a plethora of
ars, shops, and restaurants. If you are visiting with your boat, Bridgewater Channel
the place to moor or beach your craft so you can socialize with other tourists, grab a
rink at a nearby bar, or work on your tan. There are several boat-in restaurants right
n Bridgewater Channel. The channel is swimmable, but you might as well head to
e shore of the lake to swim without the abundance of boat traffic.

lay a Round of Golf at Bridgewater Links Golf Course: This beautiful golf course
located right next to the London Bridge, with awesome views of the bridge, Lake
avasu, and the surrounding mountains.

ake a Boat Tour of Lake Havasu: If you've come all the way to Lake Havasu, you
mply have to get out on the water, and if you don't have your own boat, you can

asily sign up for a boat tour of the lake. There are several boat tour options right near
ondon Bridge.

ent a Kayak and Paddle Thomson Bay and Lake Havasu: If jetting around in a
owerboat isn't quite your speed, you can rent a kayak from Beach Shack Rentals,
hich sits right in London Bridge Beach, within walking distance from London
ridge. They are open from March to October and have kayaks, paddleboards, jet
kis, pontoon boats, and even beach chairs and umbrellas for rent. get busy exploring
hompson Bay, Bridgewater Channel, and Lake Havasu.

og, Cycle, or Walk the Island Trail: The Island Jogging Path is a 3.6-mile loop that
rcles the island on a paved path. It's a great place for jogging or biking, but there
n't a lot of shade, so it's best tackled early in the morning or later in the evening. It's
n easy walk, bike ride, or drive from London Bridge.

« I travel not to go anywhere but to go. I travel for travel's sake. »
- Robert Louis Stevenson

DATE(S) VISITED:

WEATHER:

☐ ☐ ☐ ☐ ☐

SEASON:

☐ ☐ ☐ ☐

COMPANIONS:

_____

_____

_____

_____

SPECIAL MEMORIES:

_____

_____

_____

_____

_____

_____

_____

_____

_____

_____

SIGHTS:

_____

_____

_____

_____

_____

_____

_____

_____

_____

NOTES:

_____

_____

_____

_____

_____

_____

_____

_____

_____

PHOTOS, STAMPS:

RATING: / 10   **WILL RETURN?**   YES / NO

PHOTO CREDITS

CAN WE ASK YOU FOR A FAVOR?

We are constantly striving to provide the ideal experience for our customers, and your input helps us to define that experience. So we kindly ask you when you have free time to take a minute to post a review on Amazon. Even if it's only a sentence or two (although the longer the better!) It will be very helpful, as reviews are the lifeblood of any publisher's career. For a humble group of travelers and publishers like us under the name of Wanderstate, getting reviews means the world to us.

TO LEAVE A REVIEW, JUST SCAN THE QR-CODE BELOW:

OR YOU CAN GO TO:

amazon.com/review/create-review/